THE INNER SEVEN

The History of Seven Unique
American Combat "Aces"
of
World War II and Korea

by
William E. Oliver
with
Dwight L. Lorenz

Turner Publishing Company

Co-published by Turner Publishing Company
and Mark A. Thompson, Associate Publisher

Pre-Press work by M. T. Publishing Company, Inc.
Graphic Designer: Diana F. Butcher

Author: William E. Oliver

Library of Congress Catalog
Card No. 99-70975

ISBN: 978-1-68162-127-2

Contents

Introduction

The book which you are about to read is based upon the lives and ex ploits of seven extraordinary citizens who answered the call to military duty during World War II. Each became a combat aviator and none knew, or could imagine, that they would again be called upon a relatively short time later to participate in yet another armed conflict in a theater located on the other side of the globe and with a totally different enemy. None of the seven could have suspected that the combat record compiled in Korea when added to that compiled in World War II would isolate them as the only seven of many thousands of aviators who would qualify for inclusion in the annals of history as "The Inner Seven".

Many books of historical value have been written about our past wars. Several encompass entire theaters, specific battles, single individuals or various combinations thereof, particularly as relate to the geopolitical or geographical conflict under the author's consideration. This text, however, examines the recorded combat exploits of seven aviators who became "Aces" while flying piston driven aircraft during World War II, and then became "Jet Aces" during the Korea War. The title, "The Inner Seven" refers to the fact that these were the only seven aviators in our military history to have earned this status—and will, in all probability, be the only ones ever to do so.

Of added significance is the fact that the life history of each of "The Inner Seven" is an important part of the personalized chapter of this historical document which is devoted to him. Of importance is the revelation that there is no socioeconomic "form" which molds heroes, nor is there a military school which produces extraordinary combatants. "The Inner Seven" were selected for immortalization as the result of their individual and collective contributions to the aerial combat portion of the war effort, in two totally different types of aircraft, and to serve as positive examples for those who will follow in the field of military aviation.

"The Inner Seven" did not only excel in the destruction of enemy aircraft and materiel. During each combat assignment they also provided training and coaching to the newly assigned aviators in their organizations. With the exception of one, they survived extremely brutal periods of aerial combat in two theaters under much less than ideal operating circumstances, and went on to make major contributions to the United States Air Force and Marine Corps during their post war service.

As of this writing, only two of "The Inner Seven" are still alive. However, it is certain that the examples of airmanship and daring, and the attitude, tactics and techniques developed, applied by, and attributed to, these valiant airmen will endure the test of posterity——to the benefit of the present and all future generations.

Dedication

I had the rare opportunity to meet six of "The Inner Seven", to establish a mutual friendship, and to interview each at great length. These memorable occasions were recorded on audio tape and provided the basis for the content of this historical text.

This book is dedicated to "The Inner Seven" military aviators who committed their lives to the defense of our country:

Lieutenant Colonel John F. "Jack" Bolt, United States Marine Corps, Retired, a soft-spoken gentleman of the South whose friendship is treasured.

Lieutenant Colonel George A. Davis, Jr., United States Air Force, who was killed in action during the Korean War and posthumously awarded our country's highest military decoration——The Congressional Medal of Honor.

Colonel Francis S. "Gabby" Gabreski, United States Air Force, Retired, our country's highest scoring living "Ace" whose official records reflect credit for the destruction of 34.5 enemy aircraft. "Gabby" has always been ready, willing, and able to help with the completion of this book.

Colonel Vermont "Gary" Garrison, United States Air Force, Retired, to whom one listened because he was a natural leader.

Colonel James P. "Jim" Hagerstrom, United States Air Force, Retired, an intense, sincere, gracious individual.

Brigadier General Harrison R. "Harry" Thyng, United States Air Force, Retired, a great leader who was respectfully and enthusiastically followed without question or hesitation by all who served under his command.

Colonel William T. "Whiz" or "Bill" Whisner, United States Air Force, Retired, a delight to be with and also always willing to assist with the completion of this book

Also, to Tom Ivie, a long time friend who was with me at the beginning of my quest to gather information and prepare the document which has become this tribute to "The Inner Seven," and to Dwight Lorenz, a new friend, who was irreplaceable in the completion of the manuscript and thus the realization of my ultimate dream.

Foreward

Before you read this foreward, please stop.
Read the prologue, then the text, then the epilogue.
Now come back to the foreward.

I ask you to think for yourself. After reading of their exploits, after trying to imagine yourself doing what they did, feeling what they felt, living each day as they did, do you really know and understand the men about whom this volume is written? Can you visualize them as a friend, perhaps the man who married a girl you knew in high school? Maybe you think they're so unique and move in such distant circles that had your lives crossed when they were all alive you would have felt timid about saying hello or presenting yourself.

Well, let me tell you. They were indeed unique, but you would have never known that if you had not known their stories. They were the guy next door mowing his lawn–the man down the street with six kids–the father who stood up at the PTA meeting and asked the same question you wanted to ask–the fellow out on the golf course who struggled to break ninety, never did, but like you, kept trying.

So what was it? How did each of these men differ from the thousands of others who were in the same situation, fought the same enemies, had had the same training, went through the same battles, but didn't achieve the same results?

Don't feel put upon because I ask these questions. Eminent scholars, mighty psychiatrists, four star generals, pundits, writers, laymen–all have asked the same question–what made these seven different?

Some of the reasons are obvious. Each man was in the right place at the right time. Each found opportunity and took full advantage of it. Each possessed outstanding hand-eye coordination and superb flying skill. Each was a natural aerial marksman with a heightened sense of spatial orientation and situational awareness.

Given all that, we still don't really know what made these seven stand out. Plenty of our pilots possessed the same attributes and flying skills. Many of them were top dogs in their state-side squadrons, out-shooting, out-bombing, and out-maneuvering their contemporaries with consummate ease. But something seemed to lack when these top dogs went into combat. I'm not implying timidity or reluctance to engage the enemy. Nor am I ignoring the basic factor of opportunity. But the fact remains, in almost every fighter squadron two or three of the thirty-odd pilots are stand-outs. The majority are excellent. One or two are at the bottom of the pecking order of skill, yet they too are capable and fine fighter pilots.

Think again about these seven. I knew three of them well, and the other three Air Force men were acquaintances. Not one of them was a fire breathing hell for leather personality. Had you met them I guarantee you would have liked them as friends. So what was the difference? Some may quarrel with my assessment, but I'll only listen to those of you who have been there, and I doubt if any of you can change my mind.

Given all the skills, attributes, and opportunities each of these seven enjoyed, beyond that and deep down it was a matter of fearless pride and indomitable desire that drove each man to excel. And though you may find this hard to accept, each in his own way was prudent. I say that in the sense that it was often prudent to attack rather than disengage; always, it was prudent to know your enemy, to study and mark his habits, his strengths, and weaknesses. Prudence kept you alive.

Going back to situational awareness, look again at the description of some of the aerial battles in this volume. Put yourself in the cockpit. Now try to visualize a sphere of sky containing a swirling mass of fighter aircraft whose three dimensional movements are limited only by the thin blue sky above, the surface of the earth below, and the ability of each aircraft to climb, dive and turn within that sphere. The very best of these combatants, friend and foe, are aware of each aircraft within his maneuvering envelope. If he sees an enemy coming at him, he knows immediately whether or not that machine is a threat and for how many seconds he will continue to be so. If another bandit is seen out at three o'clock at a certain distance, can and will he turn into you and achieve a firing position? How many seconds do you have to fire at the machine you are engaging before that other pilot out to your right is a threat to you? Is that Me 109 up there at your four o'clock a threat? What are his maneuvering parameters? Where is he most likely to be five seconds from now? Where is your own wingman? Is he still with you? Is he vulnerable to attack? Has he been forced to break off and engage on his own? Are you in a position to turn and dive at an enemy down at your right front without running into your own people? Remember, in a mid-air collision it doesn't matter whose side you're on, and a collision is even more deadly than bullets.

All of these considerations occur within split seconds, and the situation changes with rapid volatility. The men you have read about were each masters at assessing the aerial battle situation and acting upon those lightning-like decisions–and sometimes the decision was to get the hell out of there and come back the next day, knowing the war wasn't going to be won in one skirmish, or by the destruction of one enemy aircraft at the expense of some of your own troops.

I hope I've given you food for thought and, far more than that, I hope that my words portray the deep respect and total admiration I feel for the splendid, "INNER SEVEN".

Robin Olds
B.G. USAF (Reti)

Acknowledgments

A very special, "Thank you!" is extended to the following individuals and organizations responsible for providing the supporting details and historical data which greatly added to the accuracy and depth of the text, and thus materially contributed to the publication of this book.

• Colonel Ray F. Toliver, USAF, Retired, Oceanside, California, a good friend and resource advisor.
• Lieutenant Colonel David "Gail" Underwood, AUS, Retired, Gresham, Oregon, for the boxes sent.
• Mr. Tom Ivie of Southgate, Kentucky, who was with me in the early days of pertinent historical research.
• The Air University's Albert Simpson Historical Research Center, Maxwell Air Force Base
• Mr. Alex M. Robertson, Norton Air Force Base
• Jeannine McDonald, Houston, Texas
• Fairchild Republic Company
• Lieutenant James M. Prothro, Lubbock PD
• Colonel William Littlefield, United States Air Force Reserve, Retired
• Mr. Richard DeBruin, Milwaukee, Wisconsin, 352nd Fighter Group Historian
• Headquarters, 5th Air Force, Yokota Air Force Base, Japan
• Mr. Henry Sakaida
• Mr. Robert H. Powell, Jr., 352nd Fighter Group
• Lieutenant Colonel Matthew Henrikson, United States Air Force, Retired, Annandale, Virginia
• Technical Sergeant Robert Crawford, United States Air Force History Support Office, Washington, D.C.
• Mr. Todd Baker, Office of Naval Aviation History
• Ms. Pearlie Draughn, United States Air Force Association
• Colonel Clement E. Bellion, United States Air Force, Retired, Order of Daedalians
• Colonel Paul Smith, United States Air Force, Retired, Derry, New Hampshire
• Terry Henrikson, Madison, Alabama
• Mr. Sam Sox, 352nd Fighter Group
• Master Sergeant Vincent Gutschalk, United States Air Force, Retired
• George W. Cochern Ph.D., (former USAF Captain)
for the excellent maps used in my book.
• Staff of the National Personnel Records Center, St. Louis, Missouri

Prologue

United States involvement in World War II extended from 7 December 1941 through 14 August 1946. The war in Korea, also referred to as the "Korea War," "Korean War," and "Korean Conflict," started on 25 June 1950 when the North Korean Army invaded South Korea, and terminated with an armistice on 27 July 1953. During World War II the United States Army Air Force was the branch of the service responsible for air superiority, strategic and tactical bombing, behind the lines interdiction, and the close air support of ground forces.

As a bit of background, the Army Air Service was renamed Army Air Corps in 1926. On 20 June 1941 the title of Air Corps was changed to Army Air Forces. In 1947 the Army Air Force was made a separate service and redesignated the United States Air Force with the responsibility of continuing the missions stated above. Usage of the designation, "Army Air Corps" extended well beyond the conversion date to "Air Forces" throughout WW II. Thus the terms are found intermixed throughout this book as reflected in official and personal records and reports. It is suspected that the popular Army Air Corps march and song played a major role in this continued usage. Records dated as late as 1945 carried the Army Air Corps or Air Corps designation.

One of the aviators who comprise "The Inner Seven" served in North Africa, two in the European Theater, one was transferred from the Pacific for combat duty in the European Theater and three were assigned to the Pacific Theater during World War II. They were again called upon for aerial combat duty in Korea. One was a Marine Corps aviator and the other six were members of the U.S. Army Air Force, later the U.S. Air Force.

Each had achieved "Ace" status when credited with the aerial destruction of five enemy aircraft and had lived to significantly add to that number, with additional credits for enemy aircraft destroyed on the ground and the number of "probable" aircraft destroyed as the degree of damage they had inflicted in aerial combat was such that it was doubtful that the enemy aircraft could survive. Each event was confirmed by a second aviator who observed the action, or recorded on film, in order to be officially recognized. There was also a "damaged" category which reflected the fact that an enemy aircraft had been "hit," but not to the extent required of the other categories.

Each of the aviators selected for immortalization as a member of the "Inner Seven" was the epitome of what one considers the "American Fighting Man." Of interest is their diversity of background and commonality of dedication and purpose. They learned combat skills quickly and calmly honed and applied this new expertise against a formidable enemy when so committed. It should be emphasized that at the onset of World War II the Army Air Corps was a small organization with very few combat-experienced pilots to oppose an enemy which was equipped with more modern aircraft and flown by highly experienced pilots. Rapid American mobilization for war saw the induction and training of thousands of young aviators and the rapid development and production of progressively more modern combat aircraft.

The air war over the North African, European, and Pacific Theaters pitted our "Inner Seven" against a formidable and highly respected foe which they met with valor, calm deliberation, exceptional airmanship, and rare courage. These same attributes were applied in Korea when the time came for them to once again participate in the fight for freedom.

This text is devoted to "The Inner Seven" and provides an important record of the only seven heroic aviators who are unique in American Aviation History, and who will so remain in posterity.

1st Lieutenant John F. Bolt at Vella Lavella. Source: Courtesy US Marine Corps

Chapter 1
Lieutenant Colonel John F. Bolt

John Franklin Bolt was born on the 19th of May, 1921, in Laurens, South Carolina. His father, Thomas Crews Bolt, moved the family to Sanford, Florida, in 1924 where John attended the local schools. It was during this period that he was nicknamed "Jack" by his friends and family. Jack had his eye on a college degree and found part time work after school and on weekends at various businesses until his freshman year when he took a regular job and started working thirty to forty hours per week in a local creamery. Despite his work, school and study schedules, Jack made time available to pursue membership in the Boy Scouts, rising to the rank of Star Scout. He graduated from Sanford High School in June of 1939 with the honor of having been elected Class President during both his junior and senior years. One could easily classify Jack as a modest, hard working, "All American" youngster.

With the money he had saved from the jobs he held in Sanford, Jack enrolled in the University of Florida and selected a curriculum which would lead to a degree in accounting. He became an Honor Student by maintaining an "A" average and was elected to membership in Phi Eta Sigma, an honorary scholastic fraternity. He also joined the Alpha Tau Omega social fraternity.

Jack's younger brother, Bruce, entered the University of Florida after graduating from high school, and it soon became apparent that it would be financially impossible for the senior Bolts to maintain two sons in college. In deference to his younger brother, Jack enlisted in the U.S. Navy in July of 1941 and also made application for the Navy Flight Training Program. He was called to active duty in November of 1941, selected for the Flight Training Program, and assigned to the Atlanta Naval Air Station (NAS) in Atlanta, Georgia, for induction processing and training. Jack reported to his new duty station in February of 1942. It was during this time that Jack started dating a young lady from his hometown of Sanford by the name of Dorothy E. Wiggins who was attending college in nearby Athens. This relationship turned into a courtship which was culminated in marriage—two years later. After successful completion of his Atlanta training phase, Bolt was transferred to Jacksonville NAS for Basic Flight Training in the SNJ (AT-6) aircraft and was also qualified in the Navy's N3N. Graduation took place in May of 1942, and his next assignment took him to Opa Locka NAS in Miami, Florida, to undergo Advanced Training in an aircraft designated the F3F, an obsolete biplane fighter, which was the Navy's advanced trainer at that time.

He successfully completed Advanced Training on 18 July 1942, which was highlighted by his designation as a Naval Aviator, the "pinning on of his wings", and commission as Second Lieutenant John F. Bolt, United States Marine Corps. Lt. Bolt was then transferred to Green Cove Springs, Florida, where he performed the duties of Cadet Training Instructor. Jack remained at Green Cove until December of 1942, at which time the element of the Naval Training Command to which he belonged was deactivated. He then was sent through Advanced Training in the Grumman F4F "Wildcat," the Navy's first line aircraft carrier fighter plane. This course consisted of classroom instruction and sixty hours of flight training.

Jack's F4F class was sent to Glencoe, a suburb of Chicago, Illinois, where the Navy had converted a Great Lakes steamer into an aircraft carrier training vessel named *Wolverine*. Flying the F4F, the pilots learned and practiced the techniques of F4F carrier take-off and landing operations and were certified as "Carrier Qualified" upon graduation. Lt. Bolt's next duty station was Miramar Naval Air Station (NAS), which is located near San Diego,

California, and was used as an overseas Point of Embarkation (POE) for Naval Aviators. He arrived at Miramar in April of 1943. All or most of his classmates from *Wolverine* were evidently kept together and, as a group, stayed at Miramar for forty-five days prior to boarding a French liner by the name of *Rochambeau*. The ship sailed from San Diego on 5 June 1943 with the destination of——— "Somewhere in the South Pacific."

The *Rochambeau* reached New Caledonia in late June after taking a route far to the south of that which would have been most direct. The detour was to avoid as much of the Japanese submarine threat as possible. From New Caledonia, Lt. Bolt was sent to Turtle Bay, which was located on the island of Espirito Santo, one of the New Hebrides Islands. Upon arrival he found a 3,000 foot air strip which had been carved out of a beautiful tropical setting. There were two natural springs at the west end of the runway, and the two streams which these fed were loaded with edible fish. Turtle Bay was an excellent setting for a fighter strip.

Bolt's new assignment was as a member of a Fighter Pilot Pool which was created to provide rapid replacements for combat losses resulting from the two amphibious landings which quickly followed the Guadalcanal invasion. The second of these was New Georgia Island where Munda was secured on August 5th, and its airstrip was rendered operational just one week later. The air losses from the amphibious landing engagements were much lower than expected and resulted in the Fighter Pilot Pool growing to the point that there were sufficient pilots to staff an entire squadron.

Major Gregory Boyington, who was destined to earn a distinct place in the history of Marine Corps Aviation, became a member of the "Pool." His background included flying experience in China with the American Volunteer Group where he was credited with the confirmed destruction of 3.5 enemy aircraft in aerial combat. He had also served a short tour of duty in the Solomon Islands. It was at about this time that quantities of the new Navy F4U "Corsair" aircraft began arriving in certain South Pacific units. The 214th Marine Corps Fighter Squadron (VMF-214 Squadron) was soon equipped with these new fighters.

VMF-214 Squadron had been activated in Hawaii on 1 July 1942. After staffing and training it was sent to the South Pacific, arriving at Espirito Santo in February of 1943. Receipt of the Corsair by the 214th required reorganization and restaffing of the squadron, as well as pilot training and qualification with the new aircraft. Major Boyington was appointed Commanding Officer of the squadron and saw to it that these tasks were completed by 7 September. Lt. John Bolt was included in the twenty-eight aviators selected for assignment to the 214th during its reorganization. The squadron was declared ready for combat operations on 12 September, and relocation of the squadron to a base in the Russell Islands was completed on 13 September.

The Corsair was armed with six .50 caliber machine guns and had about twice the power of the Japanese "Zero" fighter airplane. However, it had a greater turning radius than the Zero, which was cause for some concern. Major Boyington knew how to best utilize the aircraft and instructed his pilots to, "Run it hard at high speed and high power settings!"

The first combat mission for the "renewed" 214th took place on 14 September and consisted of escorting a fleet of B-24 "Liberator" bombers to and from their target, Kahili Airfield, which was on the southern side of Bougainville Island. This mission proved uneventful, as did the mission which was flown on the following day, since no enemy aircraft were encountered.

Within a fairly short time after reorganization, a name and emblem for the squadron were developed and adopted. The recommendation from one of the pilots that they be called, "Boyington's Bastards" was reportedly revised after a correspondent informed the group that "bastards" probably would never see print, and suggested "Black Sheep" instead. The designation Black Sheep Squadron was well received, and the next task, design of the squadron emblem, was also the work of the pilots. It turned out to be a shield topped with the frontal silhouette of a Corsair, the side view of a floppy eared black sheep in the upper l it, a diagonal "Bar Sinister," and an arrangement of stars. The emblem was fabricated in Sydney, Australia, during the squadron's R & R and worn by all upon return for the 214th's second tour, which occurred in October.

It should be noted that despite what some have written about Major Gregory Boyington's Black Sheep Squadron, the truth must prevail. Specifically, none of the assigned pilots had been or were ever to be disciplined, and there was certainly no "pool" of "misfits" which was, or could be, foisted upon any squadron, whether in existence or in the throes of hasty formation.

On 16 September the Black Sheep Squadron and the formations of torpedo and dive bombers it was escorting as a covering force were attacked by an estimated thirty-five Zeros. A furious air battle ensued and when the results were tallied, the Japanese had suffered 11 of their Zeros destroyed as compared to one loss for the Americans, Captain Bob Ewing.

In addition to Kahili , the major Japanese airfield in the region, there was also an enemy airfield on Ballalae, a small island about five miles from the southern tip of Bougainville. The Japanese could put about 200 fighter aircraft in the air from these two fields as opposed to approximately 50 which the combined American squadrons in the area could fly into combat. However, during the next month of action, with the Corsairs flying out of Munda and the Russells, the American tally was 46 enemy aircraft destroyed in the air, 23 probably destroyed and 16 destroyed on the ground. This was not without a cost, however, as three Black Sheep died and seven more were wounded in these combat actions.

On September 23rd, John Bolt, now a First Lieutenant, was on an attack mission when he and his wingman, Ed Harper, engaged a numerically superior group of Zeros. During this action over southern Bougainville Bolt destroyed two Zeros and Harper shot down one.

From the 8th through the 17th of October, the squadron operated from the airfield at Munda. The mission of 16 October was a most memorable experience for Lt. Jack Bolt, as the following details will reveal. His squadron was assigned the mission of escorting a formation of B-24 bombers to and from an important target. The mission was aborted over Bougainville when weather was encountered which made organized progress impossible. Essentially, each pilot became responsible for its own orientation and return to his respective home base. The route which Lt. Bolt selected, after breaking out of the clouds and finding the coast line, took him near Kahili where he spotted several barges in the nearby harbor. By this time his fuel was too low to either make it to his home base or attack these lucrative targets. He thus diverted to an alternate air base, refueled and, without orders or permission, returned to the area where he had found enemy targets. The route took him through some very difficult weather which required him to depend on his aircraft instruments to maintain flight orientation. Upon reaching the island of Choiseul he dove through enemy anti-aircraft fire and strafed the harbor, destroying an enemy troop laden barge in his wake. Flying on to the nearby Kahili harbor he destroyed one cargo vessel and damaged another. This was all accomplished in poor flying weather with the test yet to come of plotting a course and again flying on instruments through the clouds in order to return to his home airfield, where he landed safely. The independent mission to attack enemy targets was obviously something which the young lieutenant believed had to be done, regardless of the personal and disciplinary risks involved. After the final accounting of the Black Sheep aircraft which had participated in the squadron's mission of the day, it was determined that all but one, which was ditched at sea, had returned home safely. It was with relief that Lt. Bolt received a dispatch from Admiral Halsey commending him for his "One man war" of the 16th which, of course, was routed through his chain of command.

On 17 October, while the squadron was participating in an aggressive fighter sweep of the region, the Black Sheep were attacked by an enemy formation while over the Kahili Airfield. Jack Bolt destroyed one of the attackers, which brought the number of enemy aircraft he destroyed during aerial combat to a total of three during the squadron's First Tour in the combat zone. The 18th of October found the Black Sheep Squadron enroute to Sidney, Australia, for a well earned period of R & R.

The rested squadron returned to Munda from Sidney to begin its Second Tour with vigor and anticipation, complete with a good supply of Black Sheep Squadron emblems, and found that Jack Bolt had been promoted to the rank of Captain during the interlude. Munda was soon left behind as the 214th was relocated to Vella LaVella, with the squadron now boasting a total of 40 operational pilots assigned. Vella LaVella was the name of a rugged little mountainous island. The nearby 3,000 foot airstrip which bore its name was nestled on the edge of a hilly area which required the pilots to make avoidance turns during both take off and landing operations to stay clear of the ground. The food at this location consisted primarily of mutton and cabbage from Australia and powdered eggs and grape-fruit juice from the United States. The juice was called "Battery Acid" and was great for awakening the combat pilots during pre-dawn mission preparation.

The new base was within a 150 nautical mile striking distance of Rabaul, the center of enemy activity on the island of New Britain, one of the next objectives in the sequence of islands destined for attack and occupation by the allied forces. Of interest may be the fact that the 214th Squadron's Intelligence Officer, First Lieutenant Frank E. Walton, Jr. was considered by some to be the strength of the organization. He was also an historian, and wrote the narratives which are credited for making "Pappy" Boyington and his "Black Sheep" famous. He had been a Lieutenant in the Los Angeles Police Department prior to the war and returned to his former position after discharge, where he later became one of the top uniformed officers in the department.

During the latter part of 1943 there were approximately 98,000 Japanese "Imperial Troops" on the island of New Britain, which was of key importance to the Japanese. Its significance included one of the finest harbors in the South Pacific and provided an excel-lent vantage point from which to dominate the group of Solomon Islands to the south. Rabaul boasted five airfields in its vicinity, four of which were arranged to protect likely approaches against land attack. Up to 400 enemy fighter aircraft from these bases could be committed to repulse allied attacks from the air, sea, or land.

Black Sheep operations from Vella LaVella were concentrated on the Rabaul area. The first time the squadron attacked Rabaul the harbor was filled with shipping which included cruisers and destroyers. Unfortunately, there is no damage or action data available regard-ing this mission. On 23 December VMF-214 Squadron provided a flight of 16 Corsairs as part of a formation of 120 bomber and fighter escort aircraft with the mission of attacking Rabaul, twenty-four B-24s of which were directed to bomb the city and harbor. One of the 214ths Section Leaders on this mission was Christopher L. "Fox" Magee, who was the most aggressive and best fighter pilot in the squadron. Fox was credited with the destruc-tion of a total of 9 enemy aircraft by the time the squadron's Second Tour was completed. Also flying on this mission was Captain Bolt, who was credited with the destruction of two more enemy aircraft during the fighting, bringing his total to five. Jack had thus achieved "Ace" status as a proud member of the Black Sheep Squadron and was one of only six squadron pilots to attain this status.

On 25 December a flight of eight Black Sheep was committed to escort a formation of bombers to and from the Rabaul target area. Some thirty enemy fighters were engaged during the mission, with the destruction of four of them credited to pilots of the 214th. This action brought the squadron's confirmed total of aircraft destroyed in aerial combat to 76.

The mission of 3 January was a most memorable one for the Black Sheep. The attack formation was comprised of 75 fighter aircraft from several area squadrons with the mission to conduct a raid on targets in and around Rabaul. The Japanese met the formation with some 300 fighters, and during the ensuing aerial fight Major Gregory Boyington was seen to parachute from his plane over the St. Georges Channel. On the 4th of January Captain Bolt led a flight of four Black Sheep on a mission to search for their lost leader. Accompanying Bolt were First Lieutenants Edwin A. Harper, Warren T. Emrich, and Burney L. Tucker. The air was very hazy, and at an extremely low level of flight it was dangerously difficult for the pilots to tell their exact altitude above the water. The flight sneaked around the coast toward the St. Georges Channel hoping that they would not be spotted by Japanese radar. When approaching the channel to press the search for Boyington, the attention of the pilots was diverted to a convoy of Japanese barges directly ahead of them. The search for their leader abruptly ended as Bolt led the flight in an attack on these lucrative targets; the result of which was major damage to the barges. Jack Bolt was also credited with the aerial combat destruction of his sixth enemy aircraft on this date, which would be his last during World War II. With exception of the loss of their revered "Pappy" and two other pilots, this had been a good tour for the Black Sheep Squadron, which was sent on R & R for a break prior to starting its Third Tour.

Upon return from R & R, VMF-214 was disbanded and its pilots assigned to other squadrons which were based at an airstrip on one of the Green Islands, approximately 75 nautical miles north of Bougainville Island and about 100 nautical miles west of Rabaul on New Britain. Interestingly, the fighter squadrons were not committed to any air-to-air missions during this period. Concentration of destructive power was directed against ships and barges in the vicinity of the Rabaul harbor area, the destruction of trucks and other vehicles,

Christmas 1943 at Vella Lavella. Top row (l to r): Fred S. Losche, Warren T. Emrich, John F. Bolt. Bottom row (l to r): Herbert Holden, Robert Bragdon, Gregory "Pappy" Boyington, Perry T. Lee. Source: Bolt Collection

and general disruption of traffic, communications and operations on the island. This effort was in preparation for the anticipated invasion of Rabaul and the remainder of New Britain, which never came to pass.

This action spanned February and March of 1944 and found the Marine pilots taking particular delight in the successful destruction of ground and surface targets. While the formations led by Captain Bolt came to be known as the "Truck Busters," these missions were not without the danger posed by enemy ground fire. On one of the last missions of the squadron's third tour, Jack Bolt was leading his flight of four Corsairs over the Rabaul target area when he heard the radio transmission from Ed Harper, his wingman, announcing, "I'm hit! I'm hit bad!" Bolt advised him that he was in sight, closed the other flight aircraft around him, and escorted Ed back to the squadron airstrip. During this flight he was observed to open his canopy and appeared to be in considerable distress. Upon reaching the home base, Ed landed safely, and the waiting medics loaded him into their ambulance for a quick trip to the small, nearby field hospital. Ed's injuries were the result of a bullet which had entered his body on a course which broke five ribs while tearing out a large portion of his back muscles. Additionally, his legs were rendered temporarily paralyzed. One must wonder as to how he was able to land the plane. He lingered near death for a number of days, was evacuated to the United States, and recovered after a year of rehabilitation. He currently is living near St. Louis, Missouri.

Captain John F. Bolt was ordered to return to the United States in May of 1944. He had contributed significantly to the successful combat record of the VMF-214 "Black Sheep" Squadron during the period of his assignment to that organization. His calm, deliberate, dedicated approach to aerial combat resulted in his receiving two awards of the Distinguished Flying Cross, among several other medals, for his actions. As noted in the foregoing, he quickly acclimated to techniques required of leadership and survival in the combat environment and was called upon to lead his fellow aviators rather soon after joining the squadron. He was personally credited with the destruction of 6 enemy aircraft with an additional 3 listed as "probables" through his skill in aerial combat during the flight of 92 missions.

The Black Sheep as a unit was credited with 94 enemy aircraft destroyed in the air, 92 of which were over enemy territory, 32 probably destroyed and 50 damaged, with 21 aircraft destroyed on the ground through strafing. Additionally, the squadron was credited with the destruction of 4 large boats and 32 barges, 3 of which were loaded with troops. These successes, unfortunately, were not without cost as the Black Sheep recorded the loss of 12 aircraft and pilots, and 6 pilots listed as wounded in action.

Upon his departure for home Jack Bolt caught a flight to Hawaii without too much difficulty, but from Hawaii to the United States he was relegated to transportation on a "Jeep Carrier," which was a small version of an aircraft carrier with the mission of transporting combat aircraft to the war zone. Upon reaching San Diego, the destination, all harbor berths were found to be filled, and it was thus necessary to divert the carrier to Long Beach. Somehow, a party was started on the ship during this day-long voyage, and Captain Bolt, a willing participant, was fortunate to find a seat on one of the last boats going ashore.

Jack had made arrangements with fiancé, Dorothy Wiggins, to meet him upon his arrival in San Francisco, but due to the last minute change in destination, it was necessary for Jack to take a train from Long Beach to their reunion site. The couple was married in Oakland's St. Paul's Episcopal Church on 23 May 1944 and immediately departed for a one-month auto trip to the east to visit family and friends. Their return was scheduled to meet his reporting date at San Diego where he would be given his next assignment, which turned out to be his former station—El Toro Marine Air Station (MAS). During this tour in June of 1945, Jack Bolt became the holder of the F4U Corsair flight endurance record by keeping the aircraft aloft for 14 hours and 9 seconds. He remained with the tactical carrier squadron until November of 1949, at which time he was sent to the Quantico Marine Base in Virginia to attend the Aircraft Maintenance Course. In May of 1950 he was transferred to the Cherry Point Marine Air Station in North Carolina to serve with a carrier squadron which was equipped with the jet powered F2H "Banshee."

Within three months after joining his new organization, Captain Bolt had flown more hours in the Banshee than the other pilots in his squadron, many of whom had been there for more than a year. This period of intense flying was interrupted when Jack was appointed Flag Secretary to the Commanding General, a position he held at the onset of hostilities in Korea.

The U.S. Air Force at this time had one Group of F-86 "Sabre Jets" committed to Korea, and this was the only fighter which seemed to be "holding its own" in aerial combat. Captain John Bolt was able to "arrange" assignment as an "exchange officer" with the Air Force. His new duty station was Tacoma, Washington, flying the F-94. However, Jack found an Air Force reserve squadron on active duty at Portland, Oregon, which was flying the F-86 and was able to fly with this squadron as part of the exchange program.

When the Portland squadron was equipped with the latest version of the Saber Jet, designated the F-86F, Jack used his excellent relationship with the Commanding General to be transferred to that squadron. After he completed qualification training in the F-86F he flew every hour, day or night, that he was able to obtain an airplane. It was not long until Captain Bolt had more flying time in the newest model jet fighter than the other pilots. At the end of this tour of duty, Jack was once again ordered to El Toro MAS to await further assignment, where he received his promotion to the rank of Major in December of 1951.

In November of 1952 Major Bolt was transferred to VMF-211 Squadron in Korea, an element of the First Marine Air Group (MAG), where he served as the Squadron Operations Officer. Jack flew 94 combat missions with the squadron in the F4F "Panther" aircraft, most of which were of the fighter bomber type against point targets. With his eyes and flying desires still oriented on the F-86 and air to air combat, he declined the opportunity to go on R & R to Japan with the rest of the squadron and utilized the time to visit the Air Force 4th Fighter Interceptor Wing (FIW) at Kimpo Airfield (K-14) located near Seoul.

The Wing Commander, Colonel Royal Baker, was receptive to and understanding of Major Bolt's request to fly combat missions with the Air Force but did not allow this to take place. Jack then traveled to the 51st FIW at Suwon Airfield (K-13) to observe their operations. While there he happened to meet Lieutenant Colonel George Ruddell, an acquaintance from El Toro during the late '40s, who was commanding the 39th Fighter Interceptor Squadron at that airfield. It did not take Jack long to press the issue of flying combat missions with Ruddell's squadron. His request was quickly granted, the necessary "local check ride" flown and passed, and Major Bolt successfully flew a couple of combat missions with the 39th before returning to VMF-211 for the six weeks of duty required prior to the next squadron R & R. By some unknown means, Bolt's visits to the Air Force were relayed to the MAG, and it was not long until the Group Personnel Officer, George Jenkins, confronted Jack with the blast, "You SOB, I know what you are trying to do, and your chance of getting an exchange tour with the Air Force is 'zero,' friend! It would be over my dead body!" During this time the allotment of exchange officers between services had been stable at two from each with the tour set at about a three-month period.

Again turning down his R & R, Major Bolt returned to the 51st FIW in search of combat flying in the F-86. Colonel Ruddell introduced Jack to First Lieutenant Joseph M McConnell, Jr., whom he instructed to fly with Jack and teach him all the tricks he should know. McConnell had been restricted from combat missions by Colonel Ruddell due to some infractions and general, unspecified "problems" which he had caused. He was, however, permitted to fly maintenance test flights and orientations. His background was that of a navigator in the 8th Air Force during WWII who had always had a burning desire to fly fighter planes. It was said that he'd rather fly than eat or sleep, and his fellow pilots swore that Joe McConnell was the best fighter pilot there was.

A rapid and close friendship developed between these two officers both on the ground and during the five orientation and training flights which Jack flew with McConnell. Jack Bolt insists to this date that his success in the war in Korea must be credited to Joe McConnell, his mentor. It was all too soon that Major Bolt had to return to his squadron, but nearing completion of 100 missions with the Marines, Bolt worked with Colonel Ruddell to arrange his next move.

It was known that the exchange aviator quota would soon be raised to four aviators from each service to the other. Major Bolt applied for an extension to his tour of duty in Korea in order to be available for this event. Jack's request for extension was approved, and that was immediately followed by Colonel Ruddell's request to Lt. General Glenn C. Barcus at 5th Air Force Headquarters that he have the Marine Corps provide the 51st FIW with an exchange officer with at least 100 flying hours in the F-86 when the next quota cycle was implemented. By this time Major Bolt had logged approximately 120 hours in the aircraft and the Marine Corps General cooperated by naming Jack the exchange officer to be sent to the 51st FIW.

Joe McConnell had been reinstated to full flying duty by this time, promoted to captain, and designated one of the Flight Leaders in the squadron. Jack was assigned to his flight and flew his initial combat missions with the 39th FIS of the 51st FIW as McConnell's wingman. The flights, typically, were initially flown at high altitude, and if no enemy aircraft were encountered, the formation would descend to lower levels in search of targets On two of these missions, McConnell led his flight on an "Antung Tower Check," which involved a high speed dive from 40,000 to 20,000 feet, thus creating a double sonic boom over the enemy's Antung Airfield and other nearby airfields. The flight would then fly out

Major John F. Bolt, 39th FIS, 51st FIW at Suwon, Korea. Source: Bolt Collection

18

about 20 miles, descending, and return directly over the Antung Airfield at about 30 feet. The joke was that the pilots were "setting their watches" by the clock on Antung Airfield's control tower.

Captain Joe McConnell completed his tour of duty and was "rotated" back to the United States, the holder of the most enemy aircraft shot down during the Korean Conflict with 16 confirmed downings. Major Bolt was then designated the Flight Leader, and in his new position he led his first mission on Saturday, 16 May 1953. This was his 9th combat flight with the 39th, and his charge had been designated the "Hot Dog Flight." As of this date Bolt had been flying with the Air Force for about a month and still had no enemy aircraft to his credit, although he had "almost" engaged two MiG 15s (Russian-built fighters flown by the enemy). By this time Jack had flown 16 combat missions and logged 27 hours of combat time, and his frustration was expressed by his muttering, "The next MiG I see is a dead MiG, regardless of where it is." About this time he spotted a "gaggle" (loose formation) of MiGs at about 45,000 feet and led his flight in the attack. The frantic "dog fight" which followed requires some concentration as Major Bolt singled out one of the MiGs and observed a few good bursts of his guns making contact with the enemy plane. Although hit, the MiG pilot took evasive action and despite the fact that the MiG had a superior radius of turn, the Sabre Jet had a better radius of roll, which in this case gave Bolt the advantage. However, with his attention focused on the target, neither Bolt nor his wingman were aware of the MiGs flying on their "tail" and firing at them. The specific aircraft which was Bolt's prime target began climbing with the American close behind. At about 45,000 feet Major Bolt fired some more well placed bursts and saw the enemy pilot jettison his canopy and "bail out." This was the first of six enemy aircraft which Major John F. Bolt would receive credit for destroying in less than two months of aerial combat in an Air Force fighter as a Marine Corps aviator on temporary "exchange" duty with that service.

It should be noted that the 16th of May marked the last flight over Korea by Major James Hagerstrom, also one of, "The Inner Seven" (Chapter 5), and the day he completed his tour of combat duty with credit for the aerial destruction of 8 1/2 enemy aircraft during this conflict.

Six days later, on June 22nd, Jack led his flight on a mission over the Yalu River, with a newly assigned aviator with no combat experience as his wingman. A MiG was spotted and the wingman was directed to make the attack. When it became apparent that his wingman was having difficulty in placing telling fire on the enemy, Major Bolt took over the attack and during the ensuing fight Bolt was able to fire a few deflection bursts which inflicted minimal damage. Jack was certain that he would destroy this MiG 15 and pressed the attack. At about 7,000 feet the enemy rolled over and entered what appeared to be a "Split-S" maneuver. Evidently realizing that there was insufficient altitude to recover, the pilot righted the MiG with Bolt having closed to a position which enabled him to place some excellent hits on the aircraft, causing the adversary to jettison his canopy and bail out. This was Jack's second confirmed enemy aircraft destroyed in aerial combat in less than a week.

Major John Bolt's 31st combat mission was flown on 24 June, again in the vicinity of the Yalu River. He engaged and destroyed a MiG 15 in a short and decisive air battle which earned him credit for his third aerial combat victory. It was also on this day that Major Vermont Garrison of the 4th FIW, another member of "The Inner Seven" (Chapter 4), received credit for his seventh downed enemy aircraft.

19

Gun camera photo taken during the mission flown 30 June 1953. Source: Bolt Collection

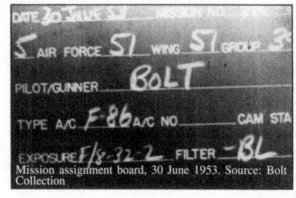

Mission assignment board, 30 June 1953. Source: Bolt Collection

On 30 June Major Bolt was leading a flight in the vicinity of the Yalu River when he spotted and quickly destroyed his fourth enemy aircraft. The month closed with Major Bolt having shot down four MiGs and receiving credit for two others "damaged" during the period. He was now one shy of becoming the 37th "Jet Ace" of the war in Korea, and would become the last of "The Inner Seven" to achieve that status.

The end of Major Bolt's exchange tour was rapidly approaching, but on 11 July he led a flight of four fighters against a flight of four MiGs in the vicinity of Sinuiju. This engagement resulted in Bolt's destruction of two of them within about five minutes, and with the expenditure of only 1,200 rounds of ammunition. On his 37th combat mission with the Air Force, Jack Bolt had thus attained the status of "Ace" in two conflicts and was one of only seven Americans, "The Inner Seven," to do so in piston driven fighter aircraft in WWII and jet powered fighters in Korea.

One must wonder at the devotion and dedication evidenced by Major John F. Bolt during this period of his career. Through extraordinary determination and perseverance, as evidenced by R&R declination and voluntary extension of his tour in Korea, he not only sought out and acquired an exchange assignment with the U.S. Air Force against many odds and impediments but also demonstrated rare skill in the destruction of enemy aircraft in the short period from 16 May to 11 July 1953. The fact that he was entrusted with the leadership of flights during most of his 37 missions with a sister service is certainly a personal tribute most worthy of note. Major Bolt became the only Marine aviator to achieve the status of "Ace" in jet fighter aircraft. Jack departed Korea in July of 1953 for a much deserved rest and vacation with his family.

Major Bolt's next assignment was with the Navy's Bureau of Aeronautics as an Aircraft Design Engineer, with duty station in Washington, D. C. However, he was detailed to the Pentagon as a member of a board of officers, the duty of which was to report on tactics to the Marine Corps. During a press conference in September of 1953, which was held to welcome him to Washington and extol his exploits, Jack explained a bit about his last mission and also went on to explain what tactics were employed in Korea with the MiGs as opposed to fighting the Zero's during WW II. He also pointed out the reason for aerial success in Korea.

The last mission: "It was about one Saturday evening when I added those last two. We hadn't seen anything of the MiGs in over ten days—when all of a sudden I spotted four of them taking off from an air base on the other side of the Yalu. I nosed over and hit them just as they began to gain altitude. I fired four bursts and a MiG began to smoke. It rolled over and slipped into the ground. I made the second kill when this other dude drifted over my way. Pulling nose-up, I closed to within 500 feet and started firing up his tailpipe. I watched the pilot eject himself and the action was over. It took about five minutes for the whole show."

WW II vs. Korea tactics: "During the last war, the Corsairs would have to make running passes at the Japanese Zeros, being careful never to really tangle with them because the Zeros could turn on a dime. In Korea the MiGs make the passes and we make the turns, especially at the higher altitudes."

Success in Korea: The MiG had the faster rate of climb, but once they got to a high altitude and were flying at transonic speeds they lacked the control of the F-86. The F-86 could turn inside them, and as a result the MiGs were taking a beating 'upstairs.' A shift in their tactics resulted. They abandoned high altitude engagements and went 'downstairs' where their performance was better—they could outperform the F-86s, given the chance. The Sabres thus stayed at higher altitudes and were able to attack first because they were on top of the MiGs. There is no question about it, our pilots exceeded theirs in experience and discipline, and the F-86 is a better plane. The kill ratio was ridiculous—nearly 14 enemy jets shot down for every F-86."

After his board duties were completed he reported to his new duty assignment, during which he was promoted to the rank of Lieutenant Colonel (Lt. Col.) in 1954. In addition to his normal work schedule, he earned a Bachelor of Science Degree in Military Science from the University of Maryland through off-duty studies and occasionally worked with then Commander Marshall Beebe at the Naval Flight Test Center throughout this tour.

In 1957 Lt. Col. Bolt received orders to attend the Senior School of Amphibious Warfare, a one year course of instruction, at Quantico Marine Corps Base. After graduation he was transferred to Hawaii to take command of his WW II organization, the VMF-214 "Black Sheep Squadron," an assignment which extended over a two-year period. Thereafter, John Bolt returned to Quantico as an instructor on the staff of the Senior School of Amphibious Warfare, a position which he held until retirement on 1 April 1962, the culmination of 20 years of continuous, dedicated, productive and rewarding service.

John Bolt returned to his adopted home town of Sanford, Florida, and went to work for the Chase Company's Mercantile Division, remaining with this company from 1962 through 1967. He had long harbored a burning desire to study law over the years and decided to realize this goal by enrolling in the law school of the University of Florida in 1967. Of interest is the fact that son, Robert, was a student at the law school during the period of matriculation of the senior Bolt. John completed the three-year curriculum in 27 months and graduated with a Juris Doctor Degree in December of 1969. He remained at the university for two years as an instructor of law courses, during which time he served as President of the Board of Trustees for his initial fraternity, Alpha Tau Omega.

In 1971 Jack and Dottie Bolt moved to New Smyrna Beach, Florida, where they had both spent summers in their youth and liked the pleasant and beautiful area. Jack became a successful lawyer and landowner and by his own admission is a driven "workaholic" but enjoys every minute of each day. He pays attention to the minute details of his legal practice, and dear wife Dottie tries to keep her dynamic husband on an even keel. Despite internal forces which drove him in combat and have driven him since retirement, John Bolt is outwardly a soft spoken, kind, gentle person who would go out of his way to help a friend or a stranger. As he was pictured as an "All American Boy" in his early days, Jack personifies our ideal of the "American Hero and Patriot" and "Good Citizen" in later life.

As this book goes to print, Jack and Dottie are enjoying good health and a happy life. The rigors of wartime experiences have been filed away, and they live for each day and the future. They share pride in the achievements of son Robert, a successful lawyer in Tampa, and daughter Barbara who is employed by *Reader's Digest*.

Lieutenant Colonel John F. Bolt
United States Marine Corps, Retired
SN 0-13522

Awards and Decorations
Navy Cross
Distinguished Flying Cross with Two Oak Leaf Clusters*
(Two Awards Navy/Marine Corps and One Air Force)
Air Medal with Two Oak Leaf Clusters*
(Two Awards Navy/Marine Corps and One USAF)

Service Medals
American Campaign Medal
Victory Medal
Asiatic-Pacific Campaign Medal with Two Bronze Stars
National Defense Service Medal
Korean Service Medal with Three Bronze Stars
United Nations Service Medal

Citation
Presidential Unit Citation with One Bronze Star

*The Navy designates a "Gold Star" as the second award of
a given medal in lieu of an "Oak Leaf Cluster."
Due to the complexity of explanation in this case the Gold
Stars have been categorized as Oak Leaf Clusters in an effort
to be consistent with the remainder of the text.

Credits For Enemy Aircraft Destroyed During Combat Actions

Date		Aircraft Destroyed	Location
		World War II	
1943	23 September	2 Zero	Bougainville
	17 October	1 Zeke	Kahili Airfield
	23 December	2 Zeke	Rabaul
1944	4 January	1 Zeke	Rabaul
		Korea	
1953	16 May	1 MiG 15	Chang-Dong-Ni
	22 June	1 MiG 15	Yalu River Area
	24 June	1 MiG 15	Yalu River Area
	30 June	1 MiG 15	Yalu River Area
	11 July	2 MiG 15	Yalu River Area

SUMMARY: Colonel Bolt was the only Marine Corps Aviator to achieve "Jet Ace'" status during the Korean Conflict. An element of intrigue lies in the fact that he was flying U.S. Air Force aircraft when his aerial record was established.

Official Record: 12 Enemy Aircraft Destroyed, 1 Probably Destroyed and 2 Damaged.

Across: Major John F. Bolt with "Darling Dottie", Korea, 1953. Source: Bolt Collection

Captain George A. Davis, Jr. Circa, 1944. Source: Davis Collection

Chapter 2
———— Lieutenant Colonel George A. Davis, Junior ————
The only one of "The Inner Seven" to received the Medal of Honor——The only combat fatality!

George Andrew Davis, Junior, was born in Dublin, Texas on 1 December 1920. He graduated from the high school in Morton, Texas, and attended Harding College in Arkansas before enlisting in the service. On Saturday, 21 March 1942, George Davis enlisted in the United States Army Air Force at Lubbock, Texas. He successfully completed his initial training and testing and was appointed an Aviation Cadet on the 3rd of June with orders to proceed to Kelly Field where he completed the prescribed Pre-Flight Training in August. His next assignment was to Jones Field at Bonham, Texas, for Primary Flight Training, during which he flew 60 hours in the PT-19 aircraft. He was next sent to Waco, Texas, for Basic Flight Training, flew 74 hours during successful completion of the course of instruction and graduated on 13 December. The next and final stage of the training process was Advanced Flight Training in the AT-6 aircraft at Aloe Field, also in Texas, which was completed on 16 February 1943, a date which also was marked by several significant and related events during which George A. Davis, Junior, received his aviator qualification and"Wings," was commissioned a Second Lieutenant in the U.S. Army Reserve, and immediately ordered to active duty in the U.S. Army Air Force.

The first assignment for Second Lieutenant (2nd Lt.) Davis was with the 312th Bombardment Group (Dive) where he was "checked out" (qualified to fly) in the Curtiss-Wright P-40 "Warhawk" fighter plane. He flew training missions in this aircraft until mid-August, at which time he was ordered to the Asiatic-Pacific Theater of Operations. Lieutenant Davis was transported by air to Port Moresby on the island of New Guinea, where he became a member of the 5th Air Force and quickly experienced subsequent movement and assignment through the 348th Fighter Group (FG) to the 342nd Fighter Squadron (FS). December of 1943 found the 342nd FS based at Finchhafen, which is located east of Lae in Northeast New Guinea on the Solomon Sea.

The squadron was equipped with the Republic P-47 Thunderbolt fighter aircraft which, although reliable and capable, was not equal to the performance of the Japanese Zero. The difference in combat losses and victories was thus a matter of skill and daring on the part of American aviators.

The introduction to combat action came quickly for Lt. George Davis. The 348th FG sent a "Field Order" for Mission Number 2-41 to the 342nd FS during the night of 31 December. This order tasked the 342nd with primary responsibility for patrolling the area around the Cape of Gloucester, which is on the west end of New Britain Island on the Bismark Sea. The formation of 16 squadron P-47 fighters scheduled for this mission took off on time at 1240 hours, with one aircraft returning to Finchhafen due to mechanical problems. The weather forecast for the target area was good, with broken clouds anticipated enroute. Before reaching the target area the 342nd was diverted to the vicinity of Arawe Island, which lies southwest of Cape Gloucester. The Japanese had been quite busy attacking American convoys in the region, mostly with Val dive bombers and their Zeke protective fighter escorts. Enroute observation of 6 Vals and 5 Zekes scattered at altitudes between 5,000 and 10,000 feet indicated that a Japanese formation was on such a convoy attack mission at that time. The matter of code-names assigned to Japanese combat planes requires explanation: "Zeke" was the well known Mitsubishi A6M5 'Zero' fighter series of models; "Val" was the Aichi Type 99 D3A1 dive bomber which was employed at Pearl

Harbor; "Tony" identified the Kawasaki Ki-61 fighter plane which looked like a cross between a German Messerschmitt 109 and American P-51; "Oscar" was the dreaded Nakajima Ki-43 which gained fame as a leading 'Kamikaze' (suicide) plane, and "Dinah" was assigned to the Mitsabishi Ki-46, an Army long range, high speed, reconnaissance aircraft.

Lt. Davis was flying as wingman (#2 position) to the leader of "Green Flight" during this mission. Upon arriving over the newly assigned target area at 14,000 feet, Lt. Davis spotted 3 Vals and one Zeke which had just finished their bombing and strafing runs on a friendly convoy and were not in any semblance of formation or organization. The Zekes were, however, trying to protect the Vals. Lt. Davis selected a Val as his target and diving closed to a range of 300 yards before opening fire from the 5 o'clock position. As Davis was pulling up to regain altitude, he saw the Val hit the water and burst into flames near one of the outlying Arawe Islands. Lt. Davis was able make a film of the remains of the Val burning on the water and thus recorded the aerial combat destruction of his first enemy aircraft.

By this time the enemy pilots had completed their primary mission and were anxious to break contact with the Americans and head for their home base. As an evasive maneuver the remaining Vals headed for the jungle tree tops in the unsuccessful hope that their camouflage paint scheme would hide them from the attacking Americans while they made their escape. Despite a 3,000 foot altitude advantage over the P-47s, the Zekes disengaged from direct combat and left the area. Another reason for disengagement could have been the fact that within but a few minutes after the arrival of the 342nd FS over Arawe the Japanese formation had lost several of its aircraft. The action over, Lieutenants Davis and William P. Wallace patrolled the area for an hour prior to returning to Finchhafen, their home base.

Spirits were high at the 342nd, and well they should have been. The day's mission had been flown with no aircraft losses and only one Thunderbolt discovered to have minor damage while inflicting confirmed enemy losses of 6 Vals and 2 Zekes destroyed with one Zeke classified a "Probable." George Davis was credited with downing his first enemy aircraft of the campaign.

Field Order Number 217 from 5th Air Force was passed on to the 342nd FS by the 348th FG. This message was received during the night and tasked the squadron to provide 16 P-47s for the protective cover of a strike force of B-24 bombers which was to bomb Wewak targets on 3 February. An early wake-up call, breakfast, and briefing enabled the pilots to take off a little after 0845. The estimated time over Wewak was 1120, and it was estimated that about twenty minutes over the target area would be required to complete the mission. At approximately 1140, while flying at 22,000 feet, Lt. Davis heard a radio call which announced enemy aircraft at the flight's 4 o'clock position. His particular flight was the lead flight in the formation and he was flying in the wingman position to the flight leader, Captain William D. "Dinghy" Dunham. Dunham quickly led the flight into a turn and spotted the attackers descending from above with the aircraft in the rearmost part of the friendly formation their obvious target. He ordered auxiliary fuel tanks to be dropped, and led his flight in the attack.

Captain Dunham selected an Oscar as his target and started an intersecting climb to meet it when Davis observed a Tony firing at a P-47 and pulled up to get on its tail. The pilot of the Tony saw Davis behind him and dove while making a turn to the right. Davis stayed with him and at an altitude of approximately 10,000 feet opened fire from a range of 300 yards at a deflection angle of 25 degrees. The Tony went into a spin with very heavy smoke coming from behind the engine and cockpit areas. Lt. Davis pulled up and climbed to rejoin his flight at 17,000 feet. Captain Dunham and Lt. Bill Wallace provided confirmation of Lt. Davis' second victory in 35 days of combat. As an item of interest, "Dinghy" Dunham completed WW II with a record of 16 enemy aircraft destroyed, remained in the Air Force as a career officer, and retired with the rank of Brigadier General.

During the combat engagement of the fighters some five miles west of Wewak, the B-24s completed their bombing mission and headed for their home base. As soon as the air was cleared of enemy planes the fighters formed up and followed suit. The 342nd tally for the day's relatively brief action against three Oscars and four Tonys was the confirmed destruction of three Tonys which were credited on the basis of one each to Lieutenants George Davis, Malcom Rand, and Bill Wallace. The following day, 4 February 1944, George A. Davis was promoted to First Lieutenant (1st Lt.).

342nd FS combat missions during the remainder of February consisted primarily of flying cover for convoy protection in the areas of Cape Gloucester and the islands of Saidor and Manus. Squadron missions during March and April were also of the cover nature but were concentrated on the areas off the Manus Islands and the escort of transports from Manus to Momote. There was, however, one fighter sweep on Wewak with the intent of inflicting as much damage as possible.

From May through August the 342nd FS flew 69 missions, which included participation in three dive bombing raids on the Japanese airfield and supply center at Hansa Bay. An additional 40 missions were flown from September through November and included six patrols between Wakde Island and Hollandia. 1st Lt. George A. Davis was promoted to the rank of Captain on November 14th. The first five missions which Captain Davis flew during December were from Morotai to Tacloban on uneventful "weather probes."

Mission Number 2-902, which was flown on 10 December, provided George Davis with the action which he had been seeking over the past several months. The squadron was ordered to provide patrol and escort support to a flotilla of tactical transports along the route from Baybay to Green Beach and then on to Oromoc Bay. Captain Davis was designated leader of one of the four squadron flights. Take off from Tacloban was accomplished at 1450, and the squadron arrived over the Green Beach area at 1515 where they patrolled for over an hour before being attacked from the rear by four Tonys. The enemy was descending and firing from a greater altitude, with their initial fire directed at Davis' second, two Thunderbolt elements. Davis and his wingman turned to meet the Tonys which caused them to veer from their firing run but did not keep them from returning for several more unsuccessful attacks. At this point, Captain Davis instructed his flight to carry out the mission while he climbed after the enemy aircraft. He flew to a position behind his first target and was unable to get into firing range prior to following his adversary through some violent maneuvers which terminated when both went into a cloud bank at 7,000 feet, breaking visual contact. Upon emerging from the clouds, Davis spotted two remaining Tonys overhead at about 14,000 feet, both of which appeared to be headed toward the Negros Islands. Using the rays of the sun to keep from being spotted by the enemy pilots, Captain Davis climbed to an altitude of 15,000 feet and started after the two Tonys, which were by now several miles ahead. It took but five minutes for Davis to close behind the targets, which were now over Cebu Island. His first target exploded almost immediately after being hit by Davis' machine gun fire at about 75 yards, and it was necessary for him to turn abruptly to avoid a collision with the wreckage. The second Tony immediately entered an escaping dive toward some clouds very close to the Negros Islands, hotly pursued by Captain Davis who was able to fire a long burst at the Tony from a range of about 275 yards just before it entered the clouds. Davis then regained altitude and circled the cloud mass prior to returning to his Tacloban base. It was during this maneuver that he observed a parachute descending from the clouds, silent testimony to the destruction of his fourth enemy aircraft. He spotted the wreckage of his earlier combatant in the sea southeast of the Sogod Bay at Cebu. This mission had lasted two hours and ten minutes and brought Captain Davis within one downed enemy aircraft of becoming an "Ace."

After another uneventful eight patrol missions, generally in the area of Mindoro Beachhead and covering allied convoys, the 20th of December proved to be a change of pace. Mission Order Number 2-940 tasked the 342nd FS to patrol the Mindoro Beachhead with 12 Thunderbolts. The formation was organized into three flights of four aircraft each with Captain Davis designated Flight Leader of the third flight. Take off was set for 1005 and the target area was reached at 1130 with the formation flying at 9,000 feet. Weather conditions were "CAVU" (Ceiling and Visibility Unlimited) and the mission was proceeding well until Captain Davis spotted two flights of four Zekes starting their attack on the formation from the rear and at a greater altitude. He also noted that there were additional Zekes flying cover for the two flights committed to the attack. As the P-47s completed their turn to meet the diving Zekes, Davis observed the squadron leader's success in downing one of the Zekes and then concentrated on a Zeke which had flown into his sights and range. Three bursts from Davis' machine guns at a deflection of about 20 degrees raked the cockpit area and the enemy aircraft immediately went out of control and crashed in the sea. Without time to think about having just become an "Ace," Davis then maneuvered behind two Zekes, and as he was about to open fire, he was attacked head-on by an unidentified aircraft. Unable to evade the attacker's fire, Davis' aircraft suffered damage to the prop and left wing, which included a blown tire and oxygen cylinder. He then disengaged from further combat and joined his squadron leader, Major Walter G. Benz, Jr. Benz was also an "Ace" and was credited for the downing of his 7th and 8th enemy aircraft during this day's fighting. The formation landed at their home base at 1315 and quickly confirmed the downing of 10 Zekes and 1 Dinah with one Zeke listed as a "probable."

Two days later the 342nd was tasked to provide protection to a formation of B-24 Bombers which had the mission to bomb Clark Field, about 40 miles north of Manila in the Philippines. For the fighter pilots this was a rather long mission as it took four hours to complete. On 23 December the 342nd was again patrolling the beachhead at Mindoro with no air activity reported. On 24 December, Mission Order Number 2-948 tasked the 342nd FS to provide 16 P-47s for protection of a B-24 formation which was to bomb Clark Field. Take off from the base at Tanauan on Leyte Island was accomplished at 0745 with Captain Davis leading the second of four flights. Shortly after take off one of the pilots in Davis'

Left: Captain George A. Davis, Jr. and Staff Sergeant James E. Walton. 342nd Fighter Squadron, 348th Fighter Group, Tanauan, Leyte, Philippine Islands, December, 1944. Right: Captain George A. Davis 342nd FS and 1st Lt. Michael Dikovitsky 340th FS. Both 348th Fighter Group. Circa 1944. Source: Davis Collection

ight had to return to the base due to a leaking belly fuel tank. The formation approached
lark Field at 1045 hours at an altitude of 15,000 feet. There was not a cloud in the sky
AVU), and just before the B-24s commenced their bomb run, two Zekes were spotted
,000 feet above the bomber formation dropping aerial bursting bombs which were in-
nded to down the bombers without enemy aircraft engagement. One flight leader went
ter one of the Zekes, and Captain Davis went after the other. The enemy aircraft were thus
ased away and did not return during the remainder of the mission. A little after 1100
avis located some Zekes which were attacking a P-47. He chose one as his target and hit it
ith three quick and accurate bursts of his machine guns. The Zeke burst into flames and
ashed in the mountains north of Clark Field, the sixth enemy aircraft downed by Captain
avis. Davis and his wingman then returned to the B-24 formation at about 1115 and shortly
ereafter spotted another Zeke at a greater altitude heading toward the bombers. Davis climbed
intercept the enemy and closed to within 200 yards before opening fire from a position on
is enemy's rear. He saw some pieces fly off the aircraft as the result of his bullet strikes,
llowed almost immediately by the aircraft bursting into flame and entering a fatal spin, with
e crash observed and confirmed by Davis' #3 pilot. This was number seven in the listing of
emy aircraft destroyed by George A. Davis during aerial combat, and there was precious
tle time for him to dwell on this fact at the moment. He and his flight returned to the B-24
rmation in time to provide protective escort out of the target area. The bombing mission had
ken longer than expected and the aerial encounters consumed more fuel than anticipated.
ith fuel low it was time to head back to Tanauan, where Captain Davis landed with only
0 gallons remaining in his tanks. The 342nd FS had again experienced a successful day in
ombat. There were no squadron losses, and the tally of downed enemy aircraft included 3
ekes, 1 Oscar and 1 Unidentified Aircraft.

During the remainder of December, Captain Davis flew three missions which included
scorting a formation to bomb the Japanese base at Luban, an attack on a Japanese convoy,
nd a 4 hour and 45 minute escort mission to and from Clark Field. During January and
ebruary of 1945, Davis flew 44 assorted missions which involved convoy cover, escort of
ombers to Clark Field, strafing missions on Manila harbor and Pattao, and the escort of bomb-
rs to Manila Bay and Corregidor installation targets. Captain Davis was checked out in the P-
1D fighter on 19 February, and during the balance of the month logged 14 hours and 40
inutes of familiarization flying time in this plane. During the month of March, George
avis flew 29 hours and 50 minutes, some of which were in the P-47 and some in the P-51.
April he somehow "managed" to fly four combat missions as co-pilot in the B-25 Bomber.

The tour of combat duty in the Pacific ended for Captain George A. Davis, Junior, on 3
lay 1945 when he was reassigned to Goodfellow Field, San Angelo, Texas. During his
ssignment with the 342nd Fighter Squadron Captain Davis compiled a most enviable record
f aerial combat achievement. He flew a total of 705 combat hours during 266 missions and
estroyed seven enemy aircraft during air to air engagements. His calm, decisive, aggressive,
eroic, and skillful aerial exploits earned him award of the Silver Star Medal, Distinguished
lying Cross with One Oak Leaf Cluster, and Air Medal with Eight Oak Leaf Clusters.

Captain Davis enjoyed a month of relaxation and renewal with family ties enroute to
oodfellow. Upon arrival there he attended a Student Refresher Training Course, and after
raduation on 4 July 1945, remained at Goodfellow as Base Operations Officer. On 10
ugust he was reassigned to the 556th Army Air Base Unit at Long Beach, California, just
outh of Los Angeles. Davis was offered, and accepted, appointment as a First Lieutenant in
e Regular Army on 24 August 1946, which caused him to immediately revert from Cap-
in to this rank. He received orders for assignment to the 554th Base Unit in Memphis,

Tennessee, and reported for duty there on 7 September 1946. 1st Lt. Davis was subse quently moved to March Field, near Riverside, California, on 6 January 1947 where h joined the 71st Fighter Interceptor Squadron, a subordinate unit of the 1st Fighter Group.

On 18 September 1947 the U. S. Army Air Force was separated from the Army an redesignated the United States Air Force, a Department of service in its own right. Georg A. Davis, Jr. was promoted to Captain in the U.S. Air Force on 30 June 1948. While as signed to the 71st, Captain Davis attended the Air Tactical School of the Air University a Tyndall Field (now Tyndall Air Force Base) in Florida. His duties within the squadro included Flight Commander and Air Inspector. Davis also completed transition trainin into jet aircraft and was rated as a qualified F-86 "Saberjet" pilot. On 15 February 195 George A. Davis, Jr. was promoted to Major, and in October of that year, he was sent t Korea as an F-86 pilot with assignment to the 4th Fighter Interceptor Wing (FIW).

Major Davis remained assigned to the Wing Headquarters until 9 November, and as sumed command of the 334th Fighter Interceptor Squadron (FIS) on 10 November. Durin the period 1 thru 26 November, Davis flew a total of 17 missions in the Sinanju and Uij areas and earned credit for a "Probable" downing of a MiG during the mission of 4 Novem ber. On Wednesday, 27 November, Major Davis led a formation of eight of his squadro aircraft on a mission which resulted in confirmed enemy aircraft downings. At about 135 hours, six MiG 15s were engaged in the vicinity of Won-Ok. Major Davis quickly selecte one of them as his target, closed within range, and opened fire. Davis saw the strikes of hi bullets along the fuselage; the MiG burst into flames, and the pilot bailed out. Shortl thereafter Davis was firing at another MiG 15 and observed the pilot of that aircraft bail o over Koch'ong-Ni. The 4th FIW was credited with four enemy aircraft destroyed durin that mission, two of which were attributed to the commander of the 334th FIS.

Missions flown by Davis over the next few days were not productive in the downe aircraft category, but matters changed dramatically during the mission of 30 Novembe The 4th FIW encountered a formation of enemy bombers and escorting MiGs with interes ing results. This was also the day that Major George Davis performed the "Hat Trick which, in the vernacular of fighter pilots, means the shooting down of three enemy aircra during one mission—— a matter of skill, daring, and opportunity. This mission recorde Major Davis' destruction of his 3rd, 4th, 5th and 6th enemy aircraft in aerial combat i Korea, his designation as the fifth "Jet Ace" of the conflict and the first of "The Inne Seven" to make this claim.

Squadron Mission Number 403 was flown by Major Davis in the lead of "Able Flight" which consisted of 8 of his squadron F-86s. As the formation approached the target area i the vicinity of Sahol, near the mouth of the Yalu River, Major Davis spotted approxi mately 12 Tu-2 enemy bombers and their covering force of some 16 La 9 and MiG 1 fighters which appeared headed for Taehwado. The time was 1612 hours and, al though outnumbered, Davis immediately maneuvered his formation into a good posi tion for an attack on the bombers. From his observation, Davis concluded that the firs firing pass resulted in good hits on the trailing formation of Tu-2s. In turning to rene the attack, Davis noticed that his wingman had gotten separated from him and contin ued his firing approaches despite the heavy protective fire from the Tu-2s. After four suc attacks, Major Davis noted that two of his targets had crashed near Sahol and that the cre of a third had bailed out.

A relief flight arrived in time to take up the battle, which permitted Davis to gather hi forces, which were low on fuel and ammunition, and head for Kimpo (K-14), the squadron home base. Before leaving the area Davis heard a call for help from Captain Raymond C

Barton, the Flight Leader of two of his squadron aircraft. Barton had shot down one Tu-2 and was immediately attacked thereafter by waves of La 9s and MiG 15s in flights of 1, 4, 2, 2, and 2. Barton successfully evaded the first three waves, but the last two scored hits on the fuel tank in his right wing. Davis sent the rest of his squadron home and turned to assist Barton. He located Barton over Pagun-Do and spotted two MiGs which were on a final firing run to destroy Barton's aircraft. Davis immediately dove in a firing attack which sent one MiG into the water and caused the other to break off his attack on Barton. Davis escorted Barton back to Kimpo, and landed with just 5 gallons of fuel remaining in his tanks.

This had been a highly successful and significant mission for Major George Davis and his Squadron. In but one hour and fifteen minutes twelve aircraft of the North Korean Air Force had been destroyed with no friendly losses. Davis, alone, accounted for four of the downed aircraft during his 22nd combat mission in Korea and had also gone to the rescue of one of his pilots when desperately short of fuel and ammunition himself. Major George A. Davis, Jr. was awarded the Distinguished Service Cross, the nation's second highest valor decoration, for his heroic actions during this combat mission.

December 5th found Major Davis leading his 334th FIS on a mission to search out and destroy enemy aircraft. At 1600, when approaching the Rinko-Do area, Major Davis spotted a flight of two MiG 15s flying southeast. He immediately attacked the second aircraft, and after a burst of fire from Davis' guns, the MiG burst into flames and the pilot bailed out. About ten minutes later, as the flight was nearing Naech'ong-Jong, Major Davis observed a lone MiG-15 closing in on an F-86 near the mouth of the river at Sinanue. Davis immediately attacked the MiG and fired a long and accurate burst. As he broke to the right to avoid flying into his target, he observed the enemy aircraft enter a spin and the pilot bail out of his doomed ship over Haech'ang. Major Davis had destroyed his 7th and 8th enemy aircraft during the one hour and twenty minute duration of his 23rd mission in Korea.

Thursday, December 13th, was another banner day for Major Davis. At about 1130, while leading his squadron near Yongwon-Wi, Major Davis located a flight of MiG 15s which he immediately attacked. Davis singled out one MiG and fired a long burst of accurate fire which he saw strike the fuselage and cause the aircraft to go into a spin. The pilot was seen to bail out shortly thereafter over Yongwon-Ni. Within fifteen minutes Major Davis engaged and destroyed his second MiG 15 of the morning near Songhun-Dong. This particular enemy pilot had initiated an attack on Davis' wingman to which Davis responded by turning toward the aggressor and firing a long burst from his machine guns which caused the attacking aircraft to burst into flames. The mission ended with Major Davis having credit for 10 enemy aircraft destroyed over Korea, which made him the first "Double Ace" in jet aircraft during the war in Korea.

That afternoon the 334th FIS was assigned another mission which Major Davis led. At 1552, while the squadron was in the vicinity of Changha-Ri, a formation of MiG 15s was intercepted and attacked. Davis selected his target, closed, and fired a long burst which caused the MiG to start burning and then snap to the right. The pilot ejected near Songhung-dong. A minute later, near P'amp'yong-Dong, Major Davis located and attacked another formation of MiG 15s, with Davis opening the engagement with a long burst at the nearest enemy aircraft, followed by the acquisition and aggressive attack on a second MIG which caused the pilot of that aircraft to bail out. These two combat missions, his 29th and 30th in Korea, logged a combined total of two hours and forty minutes of flying time and resulted in Major George Davis destroying four more enemy aircraft, which brought his total to twelve.

On Sunday, 10 February 1952, Major George Andrew Davis, Jr. flew his 58th mission in Korea, during which he, as a true and selfless hero, gave his life for his country, the Air Force, and the free world while leading his 334th Fighter Interceptor Squadron in an exceptionally hectic and challenging air battle. Major Davis led a squadron formation of two flights of two aircraft each on an aerial patrol mission to the northern reaches of Korea. As the squadron reached the vicinity of the Manchurian border, he encountered a force of approximately twelve MIG 15s speeding toward several American fighter-bombers which were totally occupied with carrying out their low level mission against Communist ground targets. As Davis was planning his method of attack, the leader of his second flight reported that he had run out of oxygen, and was immediately ordered to return to the squadron's base with his wingman as an escort. Despite the obvious odds, Major Davis attacked the enemy formation from the rear, and as he approached, he fired on and downed one of the MIGs and then quickly found another one which he took under such accurate machine-gun fire that the MIG exploded. While in pursuit of yet a third MiG, Major Davis' aircraft suffered a direct hit, went out of control and crashed, bringing to an end the life of a rare combat leader and aerial warrior. Major George Davis personally destroyed an amazing total of eleven MIG 15s and three Tu-2 bombers during six days of actual combat engagements. He was additionally credited with one "probable" and two "damaged" as the result of his actions.

It should be noted that Major Davis never flew a mission in Korea during which he destroyed an enemy aircraft without shooting down at least two in one day. On two separate occasions he was credited with the aerial destruction of four enemy aircraft in a single day. He is one of the distinguished group of only 31 U.S. Armed Forces combat pilots credited with the shooting down of 20 or more enemy planes during their career. In the short period of time he flew combat missions in Korea, 1 November 1951-10 February 1952, Major Davis also placed 4th in the number of downed enemy aircraft during the entire war in Korea, taking this position behind Joe McConnell, James Jabara, and Manuel Fernandez.

Immediately after the death of Major Davis, Colonel Harrison R. Thyng (also a member of "The Inner Seven"), commander of the 4th Fighter Interceptor Wing, submitted the formal recommendation for Major Davis to be awarded the Medal of Honor. This recommendation was approved, and its contents are provided below. As an additional tribute, George Andrew Davis, Junior, was posthumously promoted to the rank of Lieutenant Colonel on 15 April 1953.

Although the saga of the magnificent role that George A. Davis, Jr. played in the air war of Korea is regrettably brief, we should dwell for a moment upon the characteristics which set him apart from his peers. He was a very quiet, calm, reserved person and an exceptional leader in all respects. In the air he was aggressive, cool, collected and calculating and an unusually excellent and deadly aerial marksman. As was characteristic of each of "The Inner Seven," Major Davis went out of his way to look after and properly train his new pilots in the art of strategy and tactics while quietly exemplifying and maintaining the necessary standards of excellence required for success in combat throughout his squadron. Those who knew him all agreed that, "he had the look of a hunter."

From the author's standpoint, research revealed that had George A. Davis lived through combat in Korea he would have been a composite of the other six members of "The Inner Seven" who were interviewed and contributed to this historical text. It should be noted that the name of Lieutenant Colonel George A. Davis, Jr. was and is spoken with great respect by all who know of his heroic exploits in WW 1. and Korea, which were "well above and beyond the call of duty."

Department of the Air Force
General Order 20, 30 April, 1954

Davis, George Andrew, Jr.

Rank and Organization: Major, U.S. Air Force, Commanding Officer,
334th Fighter Interceptor Squadron,
4th Fighter Wing, 5th Air Force.
Place and Date: Near Sinuiju-yalu River Area, Korea, 10 February 1952.
Entered Service at: Lubbock, Texas
Born: 1 December 1920

Citation: Major George A. Davis, Jr., distinguished himself by conspicuous gallantry and intrepidity at the risk of his life above and beyond the call of duty near the Sinuiju-Yalu River area, Korea, on 10 February 1952. While leading a flight of four F-86 Saberjets on a combat aerial patrol mission near the Manchurian Border, Major Davis' element leader ran out of oxygen and was forced to retire from the flight with his wingman accompanying him. Major Davis and the remaining F-86 continued the mission and sighted a formation of approximately twelve enemy MIG-15 aircraft speeding southward toward an area where friendly fighter-bombers were conducting low level operations against the Communist lines of communications. With selfless disregard for the numerical superiority of the enemy, Major Davis positioned his two aircraft, then dove at the MIG formation. While speeding through the formation from the rear, he singled out a MIG-15 and destroyed it with a concentrated burst of fire. Although he was now under continuous fire from the enemy fighters to his rear, Major Davis sustained his attack. He fired at another MIG-15 which, bursting into smoke and flames, went into a vertical dive. Rather than maintain his superior speed and evade the enemy fire being concentrated on him, he elected to reduce his speed and sought out still a third MIG-15. During this latest attack his aircraft sustained a direct hit, went out of control, then crashed into a mountain thirty miles south of the Yalu River. Major Davis' bold attack completely disrupted the enemy formation, permitting the friendly fighter-bombers to successfully complete their interdiction mission. Major Davis, by his indomitable fighting spirit, heroic aggressiveness, and superb courage in engaging the enemy against formidable odds exemplified valor at its highest.

Lieutenant Colonel George A. Davis, Junior
United States Air Force
SN 0-671514 & 0-39295

Awards and Decorations
Medal of Honor
Distinguished Service Cross
Silver Star Medal with Two Oak Leaf Clusters
Distinguished Flying Cross with Three Oak Leaf Clusters
Purple Heart Medal
Air Medal with Nine Oak Leaf Clusters

Service Medals
American Defense Service Medal
American Campaign Medal
Asiatic-Pacific Campaign Medal with One Silver Star and Three Bronze Stars
World War II Victory Medal
National Defense Service Medal
Korean Service Medal with Two Bronze Stars

Citation
Distinguished Unit Citation with Two Oak Leaf Clusters
Foreign Decoration
Korean Ulchi Medal
Foreign Citation
Philippine Republic Presidential Unit Citation
Foreign Service Awards
Philippine Liberation Ribbon with Two Bronze Stars
Philippine Independence Ribbon
United Nations Service Medal

Credits For Enemy Aircraft Destroyed During Combat Actions

	Date	Aircraft Destroyed	Location
		World War II	
1943	31 December	1 Val	Arawe
1944	3 February	1 Tony	Wewak
	10 December	2 Tony	Cebu & Tabosa
	20 December	1 Zeke	Mindoro
	24 December	2 Zeke	Northwest Of Clark Field
		Korea	
1951	27 November	2 MiG 15	Won-ok & Kong'ong-ni
	30 November	3 Tu 2, 1 Mig 15	Sahol, Pagun-do
	5 December	2 MiG 15	Rinko-do, Naeeh'ong-jong
	13 December	4 MiG 15	Yongwon-ni, Songhung-dong, Sangwon-dong & P'anp'yong-dong
1952	10 February	2 Mig 15	Tong Dang-dong

SUMMARY: George A. Davis, Jr. was promoted to Lieutenant Colonel, while carried as missing in action, On 15 April 1953. Davis was the only one of "The Inner Seven" killed in action.

Official Record: 21 Enemy Aircraft Destroyed, 1 Probably Destroyed and 1.5 Damaged

Across: Captain George A. Davis, Jr. Circa, 1944. Source: Davis Collection

Captain Francis S. Gabreski, 315th Fighter Squadron (The Polish Squadron),
Northolt, England, January 1943. Source: Gabreski Collection

Chapter 3
Colonel Francis S. Gabreski

The life and accomplishments of Francis Stanley Gabreski and his family stand out in the annals of history as solid examples of how aspirations, hard work, dedication, and selfless perseverance achieved "The American Dream" in our not too distant past. It is also significant that the principles embraced by his family had a direct bearing on the sterling contributions made by Francis Gabreski as he progressed through the successive stages of his youth and selected military career.

Francis' father, Stanley Gabryszewski, was born in the town of Frampol, Poland, and at the age of 16 left home in search of opportunities which would obviously never be available locally. His first destination was Frederikshaven, Denmark, where he hoped to make and save sufficient money to enable him to migrate to the United States of America, where he had heard that a man would find work and be free to live his life in happiness. With just enough money to pay for his ship fare, Stanley left Denmark and arrived in New York in 1909 at 22 years of age. He found odd jobs which enabled him to work his way west to Oil City, Pennsylvania, where he found employment as a laborer on the Pennsylvania Railroad. The work involved long hours and required a great amount of strength and fortitude for the laying of ties and rails.

Francis' mother, Jozefa Woloszcak, was born and raised in the Polish town of Goraiji. While but a teenager she made a pilgrimage to the Polish Shrine of Our Lady of Czestochowa which entailed a fifty mile walk to and from the shrine. During this adventure she met and befriended a young woman who was planning to travel to the United States in the near future to join her husband. Jozefa decided to join her in search of a better life and, at the age of 19, packed all of her belongings into one suitcase and traveled to the prearranged place to meet her new friend. Among her few possessions was the picture of the Madonna which had been acquired and blessed at Czestochowa. The two determined young ladies accomplished their quest and went in separate ways after their arrival in the United States. Jozefa somehow made her way to Oil City where she met and was courted by Stanley. The couple was married on the 4th of September in 1911 at the Assumption of Blessed Virgin Mary Catholic Church in Oil City.

At some point in time, presumably after his marriage, Stanley had the family name legally changed to Gabreski. This practice was quite common among émigrés whose names could not be readily pronounced, spelled, or understood in the native form. The change was accomplished by the payment of a one dollar fee to the local Court of Records where the requested change was duly registered and the new name made immediately effective. In due course, children began arriving in the newly established and renamed Gabreski family. Francis Stanley Gabreski was born on the 28th of January 1919, the third of five Gabreski children.

Stanley had continued working for the railroad where he received one dollar per day for his labors. This did not include the time it took for him to walk four miles to and from the company each work day. The long hours and strenuous manual labor eventually wore him down to the point that he became deathly ill. His doctor directed that he find another type of work which would not be so physically demanding. Despite the national depression which gripped the country in 1932, Stanley was able to borrow enough money to purchase the "Purity Market" which was located on Oil City's "Main Street."

Each family member worked in the store from the time they became able, and it was not long until the family supported enterprise became quite successful. Francis' youth was centered on the church, his school, family and work in the store. It was during these younger years that his lifelong nickname "Gabby" was acquired, with his given name "Francis" only used for formal matters thereafter.

During his high school years Gabby played guard on the football team, did well with his studies, and graduated in 1938. Gabby's ambition at that time was to follow his brother's footsteps by going to college and pursuing studies which would lead to becoming a medical doctor. Francis S. Gabreski was readily accepted for matriculation at Notre Dame University at South Bend, Indiana, as a pre-med student in response to his application.

After two years of studies at Notre Dame, Gabreski reassessed his position and aspirations in relation to the world situation and decided that it would be advantageous to enter military service prior to the time he might be swept up as "just another name and number" during the national emergency which he saw approaching. Coincidentally, an Army Air Corps recruiting team visited Notre Dame in the spring of 1940. Gabby had taken flying lessons at the Bendix Airport in South Bend over the past two years but had not reached the point of "solo" flight or licensing; however, he remained fascinated with the idea of flying airplanes. As a matter of fact, he terminated flight training only due to the cost and his limited personal budget. It is no wonder that the recruiters had an attentive ear in Francis, who listened intently to each part of the Air Corps recruitment presentation. He learned that with two years of college already behind him he would not be required to take an entrance examination and would need only to meet the physical standards for Air Corps acceptance. The recruiting effort was successful in this case, as Gabreski immediately enlisted in the U.S. Army Air Corps and underwent the required physical exam. He was then advised, "You will hear from the Corps if you are accepted. If you do not hear from us it means that you were deficient in some area."

Gabby departed Notre Dame for the summer vacation with all of his belongings and an attitude of, "If I hear from the Air Corps, fine. If I don't, I'll return to my 3rd year of college in the pre-med program." At home in Oil City he explained his actions and reasoning to his parents and waited for a reaction from the Air Corps. Word of his acceptance came in July of 1940 along with orders to report to the Army Air Corps office in Pittsburgh to officially enroll in the Aviation Cadet Program, which he did. The next step was to proceed to Parks Air College in St. Louis, Missouri, where he flew the PT-17 during Primary Training. Basic Training was accomplished at Gunter Field near Montgomery, Alabama, in the BT-13, and Advanced Training in the AT-6 was received at nearby Maxwell Field. Francis S. Gabreski graduated from Flight Training in Class 41-B as an Army Air Corps pilot and was awarded the "Wings" which denoted this qualification. He was simultaneously commissioned a Second Lieutenant in the U.S. Army Reserve and called to active duty in the Army Air Corps. He immediately volunteered for assignment to a fighter aircraft organization, was accepted, and so trained.

Upon completion of training in fighters, Second Lieutenant (2nd Lt.) Gabreski was ordered to report to Wheeler Field, which was located adjacent to the Army's Schofield Barracks not far from the city of Honolulu on the island of Oahu, Hawaii. Gabby enjoyed a month of leave with family and friends prior to reporting to his designated Port of Embarkation at Charleston, South Carolina, the latter part of April 1941 while enroute to his new duty station. The journey to Hawaii was made on the USS *Washington* and included passage through the Panama Canal and a provisioning stop in San Francisco.

Wheeler Field was a permanent Army Air Corps installation and the home of the 15th and 18th Fighter Groups, with each Group comprised of three Fighter Squadrons. The administration buildings, barracks, hangars, and runways were of durable fabrication, and the occupants of this well landscaped base enjoyed comfortable and highly functional facilities. Wheeler is located approximately twelve miles to the west of Pearl Harbor and lies between lines of mountains to the south and north. The west end of the valley empties directly into the Pacific Ocean.

Lt. Gabreski was assigned to the 15th Fighter Group's 45th Fighter Squadron and flew training missions in P-36 and P-40 Fighter aircraft from the time of his arrival until the fateful 7th of December. During this time Gabby met and began dating Miss Catherine "Kay" Cochrane who was living with her uncle, Colonel Newton G. Bush, an Army officer stationed at Schofield Barracks. While at the officer's club the evening of 6 December, Kay and Gabby discussed marriage and were seriously considering becoming engaged in the near future.

Lieutenant Francis S. Gabreski and friends at the Wheeler Field Officers Club, August 1941. Source: Gabreski Collection

The early morning calm of Sunday, 7 December was shattered at 0755 hours by the sound of aircraft engines, bomb explosions, and the rattle of machine gun fire from attacking formations of Japanese fighter, bomber, and torpedo planes which had been launched from a Task Force just 275 miles northwest of Oahu.

Prime targets were the battleships and other shipping moored near Ford Island and throughout Pearl Harbor. Additional high priority targets were the aircraft, supplies, and facilities at Hickham, Bellows, Ewa, Kaneohe and Wheeler Fields, the destruction of which would deny American aerial retaliation.

The initial reaction by those at Wheeler Field, some 12 miles north of Honolulu, was the belief that the U.S. Navy was conducting a practice bombing exercise. Lt. Gabreski was of the same thought after being awakened by the noise and quickly realized the true situation when he looked out and saw the tail gunner of a low flying Japanese "Kate" spraying the barracks with machine gun fire, a stark indication that a real war was at hand. Gabreski made sure that all of the officers in his building were out of their quarters and then hurried to the flight line to see what could be done. While enroute to the line, he saw another low flying aircraft on a firing run similar to the first. The first attack had done little damage at Wheeler and lasted only about ten minutes, but the second attack was directed at Wheeler and the 26 aircraft parked on the flight line. Enemy bombs destroyed or damaged the airplanes, many of which were left burning. The raid also caused the .30 and .50 caliber machine gun ammunition stored in the hangars to begin exploding. Those on the scene immediately set to work salvaging what was still of value and within two hours had rendered 12 of the aircraft flyable. Orders were received to fly these planes over the Pearl Harbor area, which was attempted. However, the gunners in the Pearl Harbor area mistook this flight for the enemy, and it was necessary for the aircraft to stay well out of their range while on this mission. As this frustrating and frantic day came to a close, the important question was whether the Japanese would launch more aerial attacks, and was a ground invasion imminent? During this fairly brief but intense enemy attack, the Air Force suffered the destruction of 188 aircraft with an additional 159 damaged. 2,335 military personnel of all services lost their lives and 1,143 were wounded

After weeks of watching and waiting for something to happen, it was decided to reinforce the islands with new equipment. The Air Corps units received P-39 and P-40 fighters and B-17 bombers, which were most welcome, but not in the quantities required to provide a formidable force. However, units were able to get reorganized and begin training with the new aircraft.

Gabby and Kay officially announced their engagement shortly after the declaration of war without the anticipation that the engagement would extend over a four year period. They purposely delayed wedding plans due to the uncertainty of the future and the fact that she was a senior in high school when they became engaged. Kay was among the family members evacuated from Hawaii in early 1942 as a precaution against death or injury in the event further Japanese air and possibly ground attacks came to pass. She returned to her home and family in Grand Rapids, Michigan, where high school studies were completed and the long wait for Gabby's return began.

Within a relatively short period of time, it became apparent that the priority of American war effort was to be accorded the forces in the European Theater, and that the Pacific would undergo a slow and gradual increase in combat strength and capability. Gabreski was anxious to be where the action was taking place and, after his promotion to First Lieutenant (1st Lt.) on 1 March 1942, approached his Group Commander, Colonel Steele, with the request to be transferred to the European Theater. Gabreski used his fluency in Polish as a strong and logical supporting basis for this action, particularly since there was the semblance of a Polish Air Force in England to which he might be able to lend assistance in some way. After due consideration, Colonel Steele's reply was, "Let's give it a try!" The request was duly forwarded, and a few months later Lt. Gabreski received orders which reassigned him to the 8th Air Force in England with instructions to report to the Pentagon enroute for a debriefing on Pearl Harbor.

Francis S. Gabreski was promoted to the rank of Captain on 16 October 1942 just prior to his departure from Hawaii on a Pan American Airlines "Yankee Clipper." The flight to San Francisco was a long 16 hours and terminated with a smooth landing at the "Bay City". A domestic flight was ticketed to Washington, D.C. and included a stopover in Oil City, Pennsylvania. Kay Cochrane traveled from Grand Rapids to Oil City to be with Gabby and meet his parents. The reunion was all too brief, and at the end of October, Captain Gabreski was at the Pentagon and then enroute to New York where he boarded the transport plane which would take him to England via Gander, Newfoundland, and the Azores.

Upon his arrival at 8th Air Force Headquarters, Gabreski was surprised that there were only about twenty officers assigned thereto with no fighter command and no aircraft and that the 56th Fighter Group, to which he was to be assigned and in which he gained his fame, was still undergoing training with the Republic P-47 "Thunderbolt" in the United States. As an interim measure, Gabby was assigned to an intelligence position (desk job) in the headquarters, which he quickly determined was not for him. With some effort he was able to return to flying duty as a ferry pilot with the task being to deliver new aircraft from Prestwick, Scotland, to the designated unit of assignment.

He was quickly "checked out" in the P-38, P-39, B-24, and B-17 and flew delivery missions for about six weeks. It was during one of his ferry missions that Captain Gabreski quite accidentally met Colonel Bob Landry, whom he knew from their duty days in Hawaii, and learned that he was in England to form the 8th Air Force Fighter Command. Colonel Landry later became the Military Aide to President Harry Truman.

While in a London bar during a trip from Prestwick, Gabby overheard one of the servicemen there speaking Polish and introduced himself in that language. The speaker was a fighter pilot attached to one of the three Polish "Spitfire" squadrons in the Royal Air Force (RAF) which were staffed with Polish pilots, ground crews, and a Polish Wing Commander. The pilot asked Gabreski if he would like to meet the members of his squadron, an invitation which was readily accepted. During his visit to the unit Gabreski offered his services to the Wing Commander who said he would check such a possibility with the RAF Air Ministry. Gabby lost no time in visiting Colonel Landry to request his assistance in arranging this assignment, explaining that such a temporary move would be a natural due to his fluency in the language. Landry checked with the Polish Wing Commander and was told that he would be most happy to have Captain Gabreski join his organization. Colonel Landry then worked out the details which provided for the temporary assignment to be made officially.

Qualification in the "Spitfire" was quickly accomplished, and Gabreski began flying combat missions, during which he learned combat skills and "tricks of the trade" from the pilots who were experienced in aerial fighting. His official designation was "Liaison Officer with the 315th Fighter Squadron," and the assignment lasted from November 1942 through February 1943. Captain Gabreski did not record a downed or damaged enemy aircraft during the twenty combat missions which he flew but did gain some excellent experience which would be of great value later on.

The 56th Fighter Group (FG) arrived in England in January of 1943 and was initially based at Kingscliffe Airfield which is located some 12 miles to the west of Peterborough. Equipped with the newer P-47C "Thunderbolt" aircraft, it was necessary for the Group pilots to undergo qualification and training prior to being committed to combat missions. Colonel Landry called Captain Gabreski in February to advise him that his temporary duty was terminated and went on to offer him assignment to either the 4th or 56th Fighter Group. Thinking quickly, Gabreski reflected that the 4th was full of combat veterans and decided in favor of the new Group in which the members of the command would all train and grow progressively. Captain Gabreski was assigned to the position of Operations Officer of the 56th Fighter Group's 61st Fighter Squadron (FS) which was commanded by Loren G. McCullom.

On 8 July 1943 the 61st Fighter Squadron was relocated to Halesworth Airfield, and on the 19th Francis Gabreski was promoted to the rank of major and designated commander of the 61st FS to replace Loren McCullom who had been transferred to 56th FG Headquarters. The 56th and its assigned squadrons had begun flying combat missions upon completion of all required training and orientation. Details of the missions flown by Francis Gabreski between the time he left the Polish Fighter Wing and 10 December 1943 are not recorded however, he was credited with the aerial destruction of seven and damaging of two more enemy aircraft between the time he joined the 61st FS and the mission of 11 December, the description of which follows.

Field Order 198 directed the 61st FS to provide protection to a force of B-17 and B-24 bombers during a mission to Emden, Germany. The forecast called for excellent weather over the continent and the normal poor flying weather over England. Calculated flying time to and from the target from the 61st's Halesworth base was three hours. Major Gabreski led his squadron of 16 P-47s with the designated radio call sign of "Keyworth Blue Leader" which identified him as the leader of the 61st FS of the 56th FG. Take off time was 1100 hours, and the squadron broke out of the cloud cover at 11,000 feet while climbing to the assigned rendezvous altitude of 22,000 feet. The bomber formation was joined northwest of Emden, and as the bombers turned south to the target area, Major Gabreski spotted enemy Me 109 fighters diving head-on toward the bombers. From its position higher than and behind the bombers, the 61st began a descent to intercept the attackers, during which Gabreski saw between fifty and sixty Me 110 aircraft turning into a position behind the bombers. The Me 110 had a rocket firing capability and immediately took priority over the Me 109s for the 61st's attack. The P-47s were closing rapidly on the Me 110s from the rear and at a higher altitude when the enemy was alerted to their presence by the mid-air collision of two of the P-47s. Major Gabreski singled out one of the Me 110s and with a long burst from his machine guns saw hits along the wing root of his target. He fired an additional burst which caused the enemy aircraft to start smoking as it entered a fatal dive. His attention then went to a formation of fighters he thought were P-47s, and while flying to join them, he realized that they were actually FW 190s. With fuel running low, Gabreski slowly turned away

Celebration of Captain "Gabby" Gabreski becoming an "Ace." 26 November 1943, Halesworth Airfield (Station 365), England.

leaned out the fuel mixture, and headed to the west and home base. While checking his fuel status, he noticed an Me 109 attacking him from the 3 o'clock position but could not engage it due to his low fuel situation. Gabreski broke hard to the left to avoid the first attack, a maneuver which he used twice to thwart his attacker. On the adversary's third pass, Gabby pulled back hard on the stick, heard hits and then an explosion. Looking down, he saw that his right rudder pedal was gone— along with the heel of his right boot.

The situation was now critical. He was low on fuel, flying a damaged aircraft, a determined enemy in pursuit and still a long way from home. Gabreski spotted a cloud layer at about 11,000 feet, dove into it and pulled out of the dive at 6,000 feet still headed to the west. His oil temperature gage was now "in the red," probably the result of a hit which severed an oil line. With approximately 50 gallons of fuel left and the Dutch coast in sight, Gabby climbed through the cloud layer to the top of the overcast at 11,000 feet only to discover that the Me 109 was right behind him and quickly re-entered cloud layer. He was now close enough to England to call for help and broadcast a "Mayday" over the radio with a request for a vector to his home base. Fortunately, the Me 109 pilot had broken off the chase, and the friendly coast was in sight. The engine began "running rough," and the oil temperature indicator could climb no higher in the red field. It was clear that the P-47 could not stay airborne much longer, but he was now over the coastline; Halesworth was in sight just a few miles ahead. Gabreski was cleared for a "straight in" approach and made a safe landing in his severely damaged Thunderbolt, the happy end of a harrowing mission for "Keyworth Blue Leader."

Francis S. Gabreski was promoted to the rank of Lieutenant Colonel on 21 January 1944 with an impressive record of accelerated promotions and enemy aircraft destroyed. The full description of documented combat actions during which Francis Gabreski demonstrated rare and heroic skill and daring in the destruction of enemy aircraft would fill an independent volume and are not summarized in this text.

By the 20th of July Gabby Gabreski was the leading "Ace" in the European Theater with a total of 28 enemy aircraft destroyed in air-to-air combat and was also just one week away from departing for the United States. However, he made what was to be the fateful decision which changed his immediate future when he had himself scheduled to lead his 61st FS on one more bomber escort mission which was directed against the large German city of Frankfurt. The weather was good, and Gabby enjoyed the mission of escorting B-17s without German fighter opposition. With the bombing mission completed and no enemy aircraft to contend with, the 61st was released from its escort mission. Enroute to England, in the vicinity of Cologne, Gabby spotted a small air strip which was filled with twin engine aircraft and sent half of his aircraft home while he led the remainder in an attack on the parked airplanes. His plan was to make one firing pass at the targets and then head back to England. But after a highly effective initial attack, he felt that one more firing pass would be needed to complete the destruction which his flight had initiated. He led his flight in the second attack at tree top level to reduce the probability of being hit by ground fire. At an estimated 300 miles per hour on his next firing run, Gabreski was so low that the prop of his aircraft hit the ground, which caused the aircraft to "bounce" upward and also initiated severe vibrations throughout the Thunderbolt. Gabby's next decision was to "belly land" about three miles from the target area. This was accomplished fairly smoothly, but as the P-47 slid to a stop, it started smoking. Gabby found that the cockpit canopy had been warped during the crash landing and would not open. The fear of being burned to death must certainly have been responsible for the surge of strength which he then exerted to open the canopy to the point where he could make his escape.

He made a dash for the nearby woods and was aware of some "cracking" sounds as he entered this temporary sanctuary. Looking behind him he saw two soldiers in the distance firing at him, and sprinted to get out of their sight. He hid as best possible until sunset and then found and walked along a country road. There was no traffic, and in a short time he came to a small village of about eight houses. The villagers who observed him gathered to obviously discuss this stranger in their midst and then started following him. He increased his speed and passed out of their sight over the top of a low hill. The other side of the hill was an expanse of wheat fields, and Gabreski entered the first one he came to on the left side of the road. Darkness was with the Colonel, as his hiding place was not found by the searching villagers, some of whom nearly stepped on him. The villagers all left rather abruptly, and Gabby quickly moved into some woods which were not far away.

For the next four days he made it a practice to sleep at night and walk during the day. On one of these days, he encountered some Polish prisoners who were working in the fields and introduced himself to the startled group. The nearest to him were a father and son who said that they would come back. Gabreski asked if they might be able to bring a little food for him, and after what seemed like a very long time, the man returned with some bread and water. The two talked about the war and the political situation, and the man confirmed that Gabby was on the right road to Luxembourg. After another day of walking, he started getting impatient as to when he would reach the allied lines.

On the fifth day he met a farmer and his son who seemed friendly and even brought him some food. However, after this seemingly kind and secretive act, they reported Colonel Gabreski to the Wehrmacht, and shortly thereafter he was taken prisoner. He was confined to a very primitive jail in the nearest village for the night, and in the morning two Luftwaffe airmen arrived on the scene to escort him, via train, to Frankfurt.

Lieutenant Colonel Gabreski was astounded at the destruction which was evident upon his arrival at the main train station of this major German city. Not only was the station in ruins, but all of the structures within his view had been reduced to rubble by allied bombing. Gabreski and his escorts then boarded an amazingly functional street car which transported them to the town of Oberursel and the installation which housed the Interrogation Center. It was here that Francis Gabreski was interrogated by the German master interrogator, Hans Scharff. (AUTHOR'S COMMENT: A detailed account of Colonel Gabreski's stay at the Interrogation Center can be found in the text entitled *The Interrogator* by Raymond F. Toliver.)

The last week of August found Colonel Gabreski in a group of captured airmen which was moved from the Interrogation Center to the Frankfurt train station where they began their short rail journey to the "Dulag Luft" prisoner of war camp near the city of Wetzlar, some fifty miles north of Frankfurt. "Dulag Luft" was the reception and distribution point for military prisoners and Red Cross packages and clothing, as well as the center which directed assignment and movement of allied prisoners to permanent internment camps throughout Germany.

During a short stay of less than a week at Wetzlar, Gabby and his fellow prisoners could watch the bombing of industrial targets in Wetzlar by B-17s and B-24s. Gabreski recalled that "the bomber formations were lined up like a highway to Germany for its destruction." Since the prison camp was but two miles from the bomber target area, it was quite natural that the prisoners had mixed feelings and emotions about the action they witnessed. Fortunately, the bombardiers were accurate and no bombs landed near the prison camp.

Gabreski's next destination was Stalag Luft 1, a prisoner of war camp located on a peninsula southwest of Barth, Germany. Travel was again by train, and upon arrival the group of new prisoners was met by the internees who were interested in learning who was joining them. Gabby was met by "Hub" Zemke, Jerry Johnson and Loren McCollom from the 56th FG. It was comforting to know that friends were near and to have trusted comrades from whom to learn the ropes. The location made it impossible to escape, as demonstrated by many failed attempts by some of the inmates. Of interest is the fact that there were an airfield and factory within a few miles of the camp. The factory produced parts and the fuselage for the new Me 262, and the airfield was used as a fighter base.

Stalag Luft 1 held about 10,000 Allied prisoners at the time of Gabby's arrival there. The Russians were steadily approaching from the east, and as they drew near to German prison camps in their path, the prisoners were evacuated to other camps. Stalag Luft 1 was among those designated to receive the relocated airmen, and the increase in population progressively diluted the already sparse food supply. Supplemental food received via Red Cross packages was a big help, but in the ensuing months the flow of these packages ceased due to combat activities which interrupted the delivery means. From February 1945 until the end of the war, the basic prison camp rations were thus reduced to a diet of dehydrated carrots, bread, ersatz coffee, and a small amount of margerine. In time, the meat from some of the horses which had been killed was provided to the kitchens for the preparation of "stew."

On 10 April horseback mounted troops of the Russian Army arrived on the scene and liberated the prisoners. The liberators wanted the prisoners to leave the grounds and go into the countryside where they could forage for their food. The Allied Camp Commander, "Hub" Zemke, wisely counseled that the safest place for the internees would be within the confines of the camp where they could wait for further relief. This turned out to be an excellent decision as word was received that American aircraft would start landing at the nearby airfield to evacuate the prisoners on 21 April. The instructions indicated that the prisoners should assemble at the take-off end of the runway and board quickly as the aircraft would only land, load, and immediately depart. Thereafter, there was a steady stream of B-17s, B-25s, and C-46s landing and taking off each day. Colonel Gabreski was one of those so transported on the first day of the operation.

The internees were flown to an American camp known to most WW II veterans as "Lucky Strike." This complex was a "tent city" located just outside LeHavre, France. It eventually provided housing, care, and food for over one hundred thousand members of the Allied armed forces who were designated for evacuation from the continent of Europe. Gabby was quickly transported to England and on 23 April boarded a C-54 with the destination of Mitchel Field, New York,—and home.

As a brief summary of Gabreski's achievements and contributions during his service in the European Theater, we note that he was rapidly promoted from the status of a very new Captain at the time of his arrival in England through Major to Lieutenant Colonel in a period of just sixteen months! In addition to the 28 enemy aircraft destroyed in air-to-air combat mentioned earlier, he was also credited with 2.5 aircraft destroyed during strafing attacks against enemy aircraft on the ground and one "probable" and 3 "damaged" in the air. He flew 166 missions with the 61st Fighter Squadron in the P-47 "Thunderbolt" and 20 in the British "Spitfire" with the 315th Polish Fighter Squadron of the Polish Fighter Wing in the RAF. It should be noted that over 90% of Colonel Gabreski's exposure to enemy action came while performing the mission of protective escort for long range bombers during their raids against targets located on the continent of Europe. The average mission was limited by fuel consumption to about two and one half hours. At a normal cruising speed of

230 to 240 miles per hour, it was necessary for the escort fighters to fly a "zig-zag" pattern above the 170 mile per hour bomber formations which they were protecting.

The first "mission" for Lieutenant Colonel Francis S. Gabreski after his arrival in New York was a visit with his family in Oil City, Pennsylvania. His fiancee, Catherine Cochrane, was also there to greet him, and after a good visit and some long overdue rest and vacation, Gabby and Kay were married in Prairie du Chien, Wisconsin, on 11 June 1945. From July to September he was assigned to the Rest and Recuperation Center at Miami Beach, Florida. September 1945 found Lieutenant Colonel Gabreski assigned to the Flight Test Section at Wright-Patterson Field in Dayton, Ohio. On 24 October he was promoted to the rank of Colonel (Temporary) with no change in duty or place of assignment. By April of 1946 the reduction of our armed forces was in full swing, and Colonel Gabreski was offered the option of staying on active duty at the reduced rank of Lieutenant Colonel or being separated from the service.

Wedding photo of Lieutenant Colonel Francis S. Gabreski and Miss Kay Cochrane, Prairie du Chien, Wisconsin, 11 June 1945. Source: Gabreski Collection

Gabby decided to separate and accept an offer from Douglas Aircraft Company to become a member of their sales department. It was during the time with Douglas that Djoni, the Gabreski's first of five children, was born and also when Gabby realized that the status of the post-war economy was not favorable, more specifically, that he would be among the first of the employees to be let go in the event of a reduction in force at Douglas. Then, too, his wife was again pregnant, and he felt that with a growing family he needed to have a more secure future than he was presently facing. With the exception of the time spent away from his family and as a prisoner of war, he had thoroughly enjoyed the time he had spent in the service; after due consideration, he decided to accept the offer which had been made by the Army Air Force at the time of his discharge.

In response to his application, Gabby was recalled to active duty with the rank of Lieutenant Colonel in April of 1947. His first assignment was to the 20th Fighter Group as commander of the 55th Fighter Squadron at Shaw Air Force Base, South Carolina. Upon his promotion to Colonel on 11 March 1950, he was transferred from Shaw to Selfridge Air Force Base, Michigan, where he was named commander of the 56th Fighter Group, the organization under which he had served so well in England as operations officer and then commander of the 61st Fighter Squadron during WW II. The 56th was equipped with the Lockheed F-80 "Shooting Star" jet fighter which was an interesting contrast to the propeller driven British "Spitfire" and Republic P-47 "Thunderbolt" of the past. During Gabreski's tenure his F-80s were replaced with the newer F-86 "Sabre Jet" fighters, which were to become the Air Force aerial combat workhorses during the Korean Conflict.

In the early part of May 1951 Colonel Gabreski was notified that he was to be transferred to the 4th Fighter Interceptor Wing (FIW) in Korea with the duty assignment of Deputy to Colonel Harrison R. Thyng, the Wing Commander, who also became a member of "The Inner Seven" through his combat achievements in WW II and Korea. Gabby relocated his family, said good-byes during the month of June, and reported to the 4th FIW at Kimpo Air Base (K-14), South Korea, in early July.

Not one to be "tied to a desk," Gabby Gabreski immediately started flying operational missions and downed his first enemy aircraft on 8 July. This action occurred toward the end of what had seemed to be an uneventful mission. Gabreski had been leading the formation of four flights of "Sabre Jets" in search of enemy aircraft, and at this point in the mission, as fuel was getting low, he released three of the flights to return to Kimpo while he pressed on with his flight of four aircraft a bit longer at 30,000 feet. Gabby's excellent vision enabled him to locate a flight of four aircraft in the distance near Pyongyang, and as he flew closer, he identified them as MiG 15s. He initiated the attack but did not successfully close on his first target. Before breaking off this chase, he was advised by his wingman that there were MiGs above them. As Gabby pulled up, he was surprised to find a MiG directly in front of his gunsight and started pursuing this target. The enemy pilot's fatal mistake was an attempt to outclimb the Sabre, and Gabreski was able to pull in behind his target and start firing. His attack lasted until he was within 300 feet of his prey. Numerous pieces were seen flying off the MiG, but it did not start burning, explode, or show any other signs of being hit. At the high altitudes at which this combat took place, there was insufficient oxygen to allow any signs of fire. As Gabby broke away, his wingman reported that the tail section of the MiG had broken off, and the remainder had crashed into the ground accompanied by a large explosion.

The downing of Gabby's second enemy aircraft was recorded on Sunday, 2 September 1951 in the vicinity of Anju in "MiG Alley" near the Yalu River. Gabreski was leading one of four flights which were making a "fighter sweep" in North Korea in a formation designed to provide mutual support to all elements. The Sabre Jets broke formation at the alert that MiGs were attacking. As Gabby turned he saw 8 enemy aircraft attacking from the rear with an additional four providing cover from above. The eight attackers passed through the scattered American aircraft without inflicting damage but were quickly engaged in "one-on-one" combat. Gabby's first target fled into Manchuria, but his second was not so fortunate. After a series of skillful maneuvers, through which Gabby could not get a clear or close shot, the enemy pilot rolled into a dive. It was at this point that Gabreski fired a long burst which raked the fuselage and caused the smoking aircraft to continue its dive to the ground near the Yalu River. This had been a very active mission. Each of the flights had been engaged by from 12 to 16 MiG 15s, four of which had been shot down with no friendly losses.

At 1010 on Tuesday, 2 October, while leading a flight of four F-86s, Colonel Gabreski attacked two MiGs and successfully downed one of them with a very long burst of fire from his machine guns. The strikes along the fuselage were quite visible, and within moments smoke and flame gushed from the tailpipe of the stricken MiG, which turned and plunged to the earth about 15 miles from Uiju, Gabby's third aerial combat victory in Korea.

Colonel Gabreski was placed in command of the 51st Fighter Interceptor Wing on 6 November 1951. The wing was located at K-13, Suwon Air Base, lived in tents, and equipped with F-80 "Shooting Star" jet fighters. While Deputy Commander of the 4th FIW his busy duty day extended from ten to sixteen hours, and as commander of the 51st he found that this position required his availability and alertness around the clock. Shortly after assuming command, Gabby was informed that his F-80s would be replaced by F-86s "very soon," and soon it was! By the 1st of December, in just ten days, all of the wing aircraft were the newer "Saber Jets," with pilot and maintenance personnel transition training from the F-80 to F-86 nearly completed. The speed and competence with which the complex tasks of aircraft exchange and retraining of personnel were accomplished are certainly a credit to Gabreski's organizational and leadership abilities. Gabreski personally led the first mission with the new F-86s on 1 December to celebrate the occasion and also mark the date that the UN forces could rely on two wings of F-86 fighters (approximately 100 F-86s) to oppose an estimated enemy force of some 400 to 800 aircraft.

Colonel Gabreski flew combat missions as often as possible and was credited with the air-to-air destruction of his fourth MiG 15 on 11 January 1952. On 20 February he was leading his wing as the escort and protective force for a fighter/bomber mission in "MiG Alley." Gabby took a MiG under fire from several angles and through several maneuvers, breaking off his chase due to the erratic flight of his target. As it turned out, Major Bill Whisner (another member of "The Inner Seven") had witnessed the action and attacked the damaged aircraft after the colonel had disengaged. Whisner took Gabby's target under fire and with one burst of fire caused the MiG to crash. During review of the mission, after all of the pilots had returned to Suwon, Major Whisner, one of Gabby's Squadron Commanders, stated that the colonel should receive credit for the downed MiG since he had destroyed the enemy aircraft. Gabreski replied, "Well, he didn't go down." The discussion went back and forth, and finally Colonel Gabreski said, "Speaking as the Wing Commander, you take half and I'll take half." Whisner said, "Good," and the matter was settled.

One of the problems quickly noted after receipt of the F-86s was that the gunsighting system had many deficiencies. It was Gabby's contention that a system should not be installed in a combat aircraft until its reliability had been proven beyond doubt. The sights installed were not reliable in the "automatic" mode, and Gabreski found that he could do just as well by placing a wad of chewing gum on the windshield of his aircraft, which quickly became known as "The Chewing Gum Sight Theory." This "fixed" sight worked well at close range, and Colonel Gabreski's practice, as well as instruction to his pilots, was to "Get in close, and then fire."

Colonel Gabreski went on to shoot down his next MiGs on 1 March and 1 April, and his last on 13 April, which brought his score to 6.5 MiG 15s destroyed in aerial combat in Korea. Added to the 28 aircraft he had downed during WW II, his total of 34.5 made him the leading living American "Ace." It should be noted that the destruction of enemy aircraft during aerial combat in the jets of the Korean Conflict era was much more difficult than with the slower, relatively low altitude planes of WW II due to the high speeds and high altitudes of engagement possible with jets.

Colonel Francis S. Gabreski relinquished command of the 51st Fighter Interceptor Wing to Colonel John W. Mitchell on 13 June 1952. He was reassigned to Norton Air Force Base near San Bernardino, California, where he served as Chief of Combat Operations and Chief of Special Air Force Projects from July 1952 until he reported to Maxwell Air Force Base, Alabama, in July 1954 to attend the Air War College, graduating in July 1955. From August 1955 through August 1960 Colonel Gabreski served as Deputy Chief of Staff for Operations of the 9th Air Force, Commander of the 342nd Fighter Wing, and Commander of the 354th Tactical Fighter Wing, with all duty stations being in South Carolina.

From August 1960 to May of 1962 Colonel Gabreski was assigned to Kadena Air Base, Okinawa, as Commander of the 18th Tactical Fighter Wing and was then transferred to Hickham Air Force Base, Hawaii, just 12 miles from Wheeler Air Force Base (then Wheeler Field, his duty station as a 2nd Lieutenant some 20 years prior). At Hickham he served as Director of the Secretariat for the Commander in Chief of Pacific Air Forces and in October 1962 was selected by *General Emmet "Rosey" O'Donnell, the Commander in Chief, to be his Executive Officer, a position he held until becoming the command's Inspector General from April 1963 through August 1964.

Gabby's last duty assignment was as Commander of the 52nd Fighter Wing at Suffolk County Air Force Base at Westhampton Beach, New York. Colonel Francis S. Gabreski was retired from the United States Air Force on 31 October 1967 after 27 years of dedicated and heroic service to his country, and certainly one of the nation's most decorated, colorful and respected warriors. Gabby was subsequently inducted into the National Aviation Hall of Fame in Dayton, Ohio. As of this writing Colonel Gabreski is enjoying his well earned retirement at home in Suffolk County, New York, and remains in good health and humor. To repeat, he is still the leading living American "Ace" in 2000!

* *"Rosey" O'Donnell gained national fame as the result of the WW II B-29 operations against Japan which brought a rapid end to hostilities in the Pacific.*

Colonel Francis S. Gabreski
United States Air Force, Retired
SN 0-406131 & 0-46026

Awards and Decorations
Distinguished Service Cross
Distinguished Service Medal
Silver Star with One Oak Leaf Cluster
Legion of Merit
Distinguished Flying Cross with Twelve Oak Leaf Clusters
Bronze Star Medal
Air Medal with Six Oak Leaf Clusters

Service Medals
Prisoner of War Medal
American Defense Service Medal
American Campaign Medal
Asiatic-Pacific Campaign Medal with One Bronze Star
European-African-Middle Eastern Campaign Medal with Two Bronze Stars
Air Force Longevity Service Award with Five Oak Leaf Clusters
Army Of Occupation Medal (Japan), World War II Victory Medal
National Defense Service Medal with One Bronze Star
Korean Service Medal with Two Bronze Star

Unit Award
Air Force Outstanding Unit Award

Foreign Decorations
British Distinguished Flying Cross
Polish Cross of Valor
French Legion D'honneur
French Croix De Guerre with Palm
Belgian Croix De Guerre

Foreign Service Awards
Republic of Korea Presidential Unit Citation
United Nations Service Medal

Credits For Enemy Aircraft Destroyed During Combat Actions

	Date	Aircraft Destroyed	Mission	Location
		World War II		
1943	24 August	1 FW 190	Ramrod	Dreux
	3 September	1 FW190	Ramrod	St. Germain
	5 November	1 FW190	Ramrod	Rheine
	26 November	2 Me 109	Ramrod	Oldenburg
	29 November	2 Me 109	Ramrod	Bremen
	11 December	1 Me 110	Ramrod	Esens
1944	29 January	1 Me 110	Ramrod	Koblenz
	30 January	2 Me 110	Ramrod	Lingen
	20 February	2 Me 210	Ramrod	Hannover
	22 February	1 FW190	Ramrod	Lippstadt
	16 March	2 FW190	Ramrod	Nancy
	27 March	2 Me 109	Ramrod	Nantes
	8 May	1 Me 109	Ramrod	Celle
	22 May	3 FW190	Rodeo	Hoperhofen
	7 June	1 Me 109	GSC	Dreux
		1 FW190	GSC	Dreux
	12 June	2 Me 109	GSC	Evreux
	27 June	1 Me 109	Dive Bomb	La Perth
	5 July	1 Me 109	Ramrod	Evreux

Mission Code:		
	Ramrod	*Bomber Escort*
	Rodeo	*Bomber Escort with Bombers Used As "Bait" to Lure Enemy Fighters to Engage the Escort Fighters*
	GSC	*General Staff Corps (to Escort the Aircraft Carrying Senior Officers and Officials to Observe the Ground Combat Area, Presumably Normandy.)*
	Dive Bomb	*as the term implies*

Korea

1951	8 July	1 Mig 15		Pyongyang
	2 September	1 Mig 15		Taechon
	2 October	1 Mig 15		Uiju
1952	11 January	1 Mig 15		Chungsan'jongsi
	20 February	5 Mig 15		Uiju
	1 April	1 Mig 15		Yongsani
	13 April	1 Mig 15		Sinuiju

SUMMARY: Colonel Gabreski is the highest scoring American "Ace" alive at this time (2000).

Official Record: 34.5 Enemy Aircraft Destroyed, 1 Probably Destroyed, 5 Damaged and 3 Destroyed on the ground.

Across: "Gabby's" Famous Photograph, Circa July 1944. Source: Gabreski Collection

Aviation Cadet Vermont Garrison, Class 41-C, Primary Flight Training,
Muskogee, Oklahoma, 1941. Source: Garrison Collection

Chapter 4

Colonel Vermont Garrison

"The Kentucky Marksman"

Vermont Garrison was born on October 21st 1915, on a farm near Mount Victory, Kentucky. He attended the local schools and graduated from high school in 1933. Considering the depression of this period and the state of the economy in Eastern Kentucky, Vermont felt quite fortunate to be able to continue his education for two and one half years, initially at Eastern State Teachers College (now Eastern Kentucky University) in Richmond and then Sue Bennett Junior College in London, Kentucky, from which he was awarded a teaching certificate. Vermont became a school teacher, and taught at the elementary level in his native state until the clouds of war became ominous. Whether he acquired the nickname "Garry" before or after entering the service is unclear.

His application for flight training in the Army Air Corps was accepted, and Cadet Garrison was ordered to Muskogee, Oklahoma, for training as part of Class 41-G. Things went fairly smoothly until he was undergoing Advanced Training at Brooks Field, Texas. "At this point I decided to join the Royal Air Force because the Army Air Corps kicked me out. This was in late 1941; America was not yet in the war, so my enlistment in the RAF was done in sort of a clandestine manner."

Vermont Garrison signed up with the Royal Air Force in Dallas, Texas and was immediately sent to El Centro, California, for an RAF transition course. This was administered by American civilian instructors under contract to the Clayton Knight Committee, which recruited Americans for the British Armed Forces. Upon graduation he was commissioned a Pilot Officer and sent to Ottawa, Canada, for processing, and shortly thereafter was transported to a seaport where he soon found himself on a ship heading for England.

After surviving a long and dangerous voyage through U-boat infested waters, Garrison, like all young aviators, thought he would soon be engaging the Germans in a shooting war over England. Much to his consternation he learned that he must complete more training courses. During the next several weeks, while assigned to the RAF, Pilot Officer Garrison flew many hours in British "Hurricane" and "Spitfire" fighter planes and then the newly received American P-51A "Mustang." While he was training in the Mustang, his instructors took notice of his extraordinary aerial gunnery skills, and he was soon assigned as an instructor in this discipline with the title of "The Kentucky Marksman." Along with his new position he received a promotion to Flying Officer, which included a welcome raise in pay.

At about the time that Flying Officer Garrison started his new duty assignment, the Americans were beginning to form the 8th Air Force in England, and by the fall of 1942 many of the U.S. citizens serving in the RAF had transferred to the Army Air Corps. Garrison, however, remained with the RAF until July of 1943; at which time he and twenty-five other young Americans made the move to join their countrymen.

Vermont Garrison was commissioned a First Lieutenant by the Army Air Force and immediately sent to Station 442 at Atcham for transition training. It was here that he was introduced to the massive Republic P-47 "Thunderbolt" fighter and spent the next two months mastering all aspects of flying this aircraft. Lt. Garrison received orders assigning him to the 4th Fighter Group (FG) of the 8th Fighter Command (Also identified as VIIIth Fighter Command of the VIIIth Air Force). He reported on 26 September 1943 and was further assigned to the 336th Fighter Squadron located at Debden Air Field.

Flying Officer Vermont Garrison, P-51 Gunnery Instructor, Hawarden Royal Air Force Station, 1942. Source: Garrison Collection

Flying Officer Vermont Garrison at Royal Bath Hotel Replacement Center, Bournemouth, England 1942. Source: Garrison Collection

The air war over Europe was entering a new phase at this time. The 8th Fighter Command was growing in strength and capability and preparing to strike deeper into enemy territory in order to better protect the bombers from the Luftwaffe as well as to inflict destruction on aerial and ground targets of opportunity. The day after Garrison's arrival at Debden, the 4th FG participated in the first extended range mission by use of "belly tanks" and successfully escorted a bomber formation on its mission to Emden, Germany, and back. The presence of escort fighters in the target area caught the Luftwaffe by surprise, and 21 German fighter planes were downed as opposed to one friendly fighter loss.

Lt. Garrison flew his first mission with the 336th FS on 4 October 1943 when Lt. Colonel Don Blakeslee led the 4th FG on a mission to escort bombers from the target area back to their bases in England. The mission was uneventful as the bomber formation did not meet the fighters at the given rendezvous point, and no enemy planes were encountered.

During the next two months, fighters of the 8th Fighter Command scored heavily against the Luftwaffe, but for some reason the 4th FG never seemed to be where the action was taking place. The 336th claimed the downing of 12 enemy aircraft during this period; six of which were destroyed during a single mission. Lt. Garrison was a member of the flights which had no contact with the enemy and thus was unable to test his combat skills during these missions.

On 16 December the 4th FG, led by Lt. Colonel Sheldon Edner, flew to Bremen to meet with and escort a formation of bombers back to England. Upon the arrival of the 336th at its rendezvous point, the bombers were nowhere in sight. The flight proceeded for four more minutes before beginning a series of orbits. While orbiting and trying to spot the bombers, Lt. Garrison saw a lone Junkers Ju 88 flying at a lower altitude and informed the flight leader that he was going after him. The enemy pilot saw Garrison and his wingman as they dived toward him and turned into the attack. Garrison maneuvered to the rear of the Junkers and opened fire, observing good hits until he had to break off and begin another attack. This time Garrison registered good hits on the port engine, wing, and fuselage. By now the enemy plane was also under attack by Lts. Don Gentile and Louis "Red Dog" Norley, and the combined gunfire of the three Thunderbolt pilots sent the Ju 88 crashing to earth in flames.

Each of the pilots involved was awarded credit for 1/3 of the aircraft destroyed. Participation in this shared downing was Garrison's only combat engagement during 1943.

Units of the 8th Fighter Command began operating under new policies and with improved tactics at the beginning of 1944, which enabled its pilots to rapidly improve their record of aerial combat success. Vermont Garrison took advantage of the expanded latitudes now afforded, as demonstrated over the following two months. During the mission flown on 7 January, he "shot the tail feathers off" a Focke-Wolf FW 190 during an air battle over Le Chateau, France, but could only claim the enemy aircraft as "damaged" since it disappeared into a cloud and its destruction could not be verified. He then turned his attention to another FW 190 which he caused to disengage from an attack on a squadron P-47.

Exactly one week later the 4th FG flew a mission over France during which it engaged a formation of enemy fighters in the vicinity of the Compiegne Woods. The Group shot down eight of their opponents; two of which were credited to Lt. Garrison. He described the action as follows: "I was flying as 'Blue 4' in 'Shirtblue' Squadron at about 26,000 feet when a group of 12 to 15 enemy aircraft were reported at 11 o'clock. I picked out two that were diving away and started down after them. Lt. Norley, who was 'Blue 3,' went with me. At 12, 000 feet or so, I caught the rearmost FW 190 and opened fire at 800 or 900 yards. The aircraft began to smoke, and I kept firing and observing hits as I closed to 300 yards; then I saw it go down in a spiral. I broke away to attack the second aircraft and opened fire at about 600 yards. I could see the bullet strikes which caused the engine of the 190 begin to smoke and large pieces of the aircraft to fly off. I thought I observed the pilot bailing out, but am not sure. The film will show something coming out of the cockpit looking like a man. I closed to about 250 yards and observed hit flashes all over the aircraft. This FW 190 had what I took to be two underslung guns on the wings. Lt. Norley also fired at this target. The 190 went down in a spiral, and after I broke away, I looked down and observed a spot where what I took to be the first aircraft had hit in a field. Lt. Norley confirmed that my first target had in fact crashed. These aircraft took very little evasive action. Lt. Norley and I then joined up with two more P-47s and climbed back up. I claimed one FW 190 destroyed and one shared with Lt. Norley." The films showed otherwise, however, and in spite of Garrison's offer to share the second downed aircraft with Lt. Norley, he was awarded credit for them both.

Action continued hot and heavy for the 4th FG during the remainder of January, and by 30 January the Group had destroyed a total of 23 enemy aircraft in aerial combat. The Group's final mission of the month was flown on 31 January. It was a dive bombing mission on the Gilze-Rijen Airdrome in Holland, with half of the fighters escorting the bomb laden ("Thunderbomber") P-47s. Upon arrival over Gilze-Rijen, the bombers peeled off and accurately placed their 500 pounders on the target. At the same time the fighters encountered several gaggles of Me 109s and dogfights quickly ensued. When the action was over, six of the enemy aircraft had been shot down, and there were no friendly losses. One of the 109s fell to the guns of Vermont Garrison but not without a real struggle. His adversary was the complete opposite of the pilots of the two FW 190s he had downed on 14 January. Garrison described this enemy pilot as "very intrepid, and he seemed quite willing to fight, much to my discomfort." It was only after an air battle which lasted 15 minutes and ranged over altitudes from 28,000 feet to nearly ground level ("on the deck") that Garrison was able to shoot down his adversary.

The first four 4th FG missions in February were totally uneventful, but on 6 February the 336th encountered the Luftwaffe in force during a bomber escort mission to and from Romilly, France. The fighters were engaged in running air battles over the course of most of this mission with the loss of one P-47 and its pilot. The enemy lost three aircraft to the American pilots with credit for the destruction of two of them accorded Lt. Garrison and his wingman, Lt. Robert Hobert. The action was initiated when two FW 190s were spotted flying about 500 feet beneath them; the pilots of which were evidently either intent upon attacking the bomber formation or inexperienced. Garrison and Hobert turned and dove at them without being noticed and from positions behind the 190s quickly shot them down. Immediately thereafter, Garrison was attacked by two FW 190s. Hobert called for him to "break," and Garrison turned his Thunderbolt directly toward the attackers. Both American pilots saw their bullets strike the enemy aircraft, but at this point Garrison ran out of ammunition; both pilots disengaged from the combat and headed for home base. With credit for his fourth downed aircraft in less than thirty days, Vermont Garrison demonstrated the skill which would soon challenge Lieutenants Gentile and Beeson for top scoring honors in the 4th Fighter Group.

Along with his rapidly climbing record of downed enemy aircraft, Vermont Garrison was establishing a positive reputation within his squadron. It had not taken Squadron Commander Major James A. Goodson long to realize that he had not only an outstanding fighter pilot in Garrison but also a lieutenant who was a steadying influence in the squadron, and a man who put the mission objectives ahead of personal achievement. During a talk given at the Air Force Museum years later, Jim Goodson referred to Garrison as one of the 336th Fighter Squadron's "Rocks of Gibraltar" and explained that Lt. Garrison, unlike Lt. Gentile, would stay with the bombers instead of dashing off at the first sign of an enemy fighter target. Goodson recalls, "Vermont Garrison was a remarkable pilot and a brilliant marksman—one of our unsung heroes. And whenever Gentile and his wingman John Godfrey got into trouble, Garry would bail them out."

Lt. Garrison became an "Ace" during an escort mission to Nienburg, Germany, on 10 February when the 4th FG encountered some very determined Luftwaffe pilots. The engagement extended all the way from the Netherlands to Hannover. Eight enemy aircraft were shot down during this running battle, and Lt. Garrison claimed one of them as the formation passed over the Dummer Lake area. It was here that the Red Flight of the 336th FS engaged five Me 109s with Garrison leading the attack. He saw the fifth 109 make a turn which was too wide to stay in formation, and Garrison chose this one as his target. The enemy pilot dove away from Garrison but was quickly overtaken, and Garry opened fire from a range of 300 yards. The bullets from his machine guns raked the 109 and blasted chunks of metal from it; some of which hit and damaged one of Garry's wings which caused him to break off the attack. However, the enemy plane was already doomed, and Garrison's wingman, Lt. George Villinger, saw the pilot jump from his stricken plane and confirmed the downing of Garry's fifth aircraft. (At this time it was thought that Garry's score was 4.83 aircraft destroyed as his "shared" downing on 14 January with Lt. Norley had not yet been resolved in Garry's favor.)

The latter part of February was a very busy and eventful period for the 4th FG. The Group was committed to take part in the massive bomber offensive code named "Big Week" against the German aircraft industry facilities which began on 20 February and extended through the 25th. At the same time, the pilots were expected to transition from the P-47 "Thunderbolt" to the newly received P-51B "Mustang." Group Commander Colonel Don Blakeslee had finally won his battle to get the new fighter by promising to have them operational within 24 hours of receipt and was "damned sure" that this was going to happen. As the result of this promise, his pilots were flying training missions between their combat missions during the period 14-27 February. Despite the pressure of training in a new aircraft and continuing the combat routine, the 4th FG continued to score heavily against the Luftwaffe. The 4th Group pilots shot down four enemy planes during the mission of 20 February. Lt. Garrison received credit for having "damaged" a fifth. On the last day of the "Big Week," Garrison again figured in the scoring by shooting down one of the five enemy aircraft claimed during the Group mission. It appears that Garry believed that he needed credit for destroying an additional enemy aircraft in order to become an "Ace," and took extraordinary measures to insure that there was no question about the downing his next conquest. His after action "Encounter Report" read:

"2/25/44 1230 Luxembourg. Good visibility. One FW 190 destroyed.

I was flying spare to Shirtblue Squadron. We crossed the coast and not one in my squadron turned back so I joined a 3 plane section in Greenbelt Squadron. One of the men had turned back. Shortly after we had R/V (rendezvous) with the bombers I saw two FW 190's some distance ahead of us make an attack on the bombers and break down (dive). I immediately reported these E/A (enemy aircraft) and broke after them. I began to close on the E/A I was after. I started firing at about 15,000 feet at about 600 yards range. I hit this E/A, seeing several strikes and then he turned and I overshot him. I whipped around on his tail again and started down again. His engine was smoking badly now. I did not catch him the second time until he was down on the deck at about 100 feet. I closed up, started shooting, getting good strikes and I put his engine on fire. We were right down just above the ground. I hit him several more times at close range. I closed up to about 75 yards. I overshot again as his engine was gone and he was slowing down. I am almost sure his right aileron was shot away. The plane was beginning to burn more and the pilot was evidently trying to force land in a bunch of small fields. I slowed down and got behind him, giving him a few more short bursts and he went straight into the ground. The plane broke up. A wing came off and the engine stopped about 100 yards away from the rest of the plane. I then turned my guns off, looked around well and went back and took pictures of the plane burning in the meadow. I made two turns over it. It was burning nicely. While firing at this E/A, oil came back from an engine and went all over my kite. I saw some strikes on some houses while I was firing at this Jerry but I saw no people. I then climbed up and came home alone. This FW 190 had a yellow nose. I claim one FW 190 destroyed.

(NOTE: 8th FC did not initially recognize this downing and failed to award the credit despite the preceding report and film verification. The matter was later resolved in Garry's favor.)

The latest downing brought Garrison's total to 6 1/3 enemy aircraft destroyed in aerial combat and closed his P-47 "Thunderbolt" era. Three days later he flew his first mission in the P-51B "Mustang" which was coded "VF * H" (VF for the 336th FS, 4th FG, and H for the individual aircraft) and recorded his only destruction of an enemy aircraft while it was on the ground. The 4th FG was committed to a free lance fighter sweep over France and was able to dispatch 35 new Mustangs on this mission. Several of the Mustang pilots aborted and returned to Debden due to mechanical problems, but the remainder of the Group formation continued along the pre-planned flight path. No enemy aircraft were lured into the air during this fighter sweep; however, as the formation passed over the Soisson area, Garrison, who was flying in number 4 position in a flight of 334th FS aircraft led by Captain Beeson, saw an airfield and obtained permission to attack it. He was joined by Beeson and

Lts. Nicholas Megura and Bill Smith, each of whom received credit for 1/4 of the parked Ju 88s which they destroyed during their firing pass.

Garrison's missions of 29 February and 2 March were virtually uneventful, his only target being a train which he and two other pilots strafed on the 29th. March 3rd, however, was billed as the mission for which they had all been waiting——a strike against Berlin! The air at Debden was filled with excitement and enthusiasm when the target was announced since the range of the Mustangs enabled the pilots to take the fight into the heart of the enemy. The mission briefing was held at 0900 and by 0934 the Mustangs were airborne and heading for Berlin. The poor weather encountered over the continent did not interfere with the scheduled rendezvous with the bombers, which took place on schedule near Neumunster. As the formation continued toward Berlin; the weather worsened, and the 8th Air Force controllers were obliged to recall the mission. After changing course and heading for England, the 4th FG squadrons became separated in clouds, and before long the pilots of the 336th FS found themselves deeply involved with a pair of determined enemies—the weather and formations of some sixty to eighty enemy fighters. The nine 336th pilots spotted the enemy at about the same time they were noticed by their opponents and made a gentle turn to starboard to meet the Luftwaffe attack. As the opposing formations converged, the German units split up in order to envelop the Mustangs in a trap. The action began with a feint by some FW 190s which quickly performed a Split-S maneuver after their first pass and headed downward. Their plan worked as two Mustangs went after them and in turn were attacked by several other 190s. Minutes later Lt. Glenn Herter was sent crashing to his death, and his wingman somehow escaped any damage or injury and returned to the fight. At this point the seriously outnumbered Americans somehow turned the tables and, in spite of the heavily weighted odds against them, fought their way out of the trap and downed seven of the enemy planes while doing so. (This report was later changed to reflect the totals of 5 destroyed and 2 probably destroyed, which does not detract from the successes recorded by so few against so many.) This engagement was a real test of Garry's skills as, in addition to the tremendous odds encountered, his second stage supercharger failed and his engine could not develop full power. Nevertheless, he prevailed and succeeded during this mission which was his last during WW II. His encounter report which follows provides details of this air battle:

Pilot's Combat Report,   VIII Fighter Command F.O. 25
5 June 1945

I was flying Blue 3 in 336 Fighter Squadron on 3 March 1944. We were to pick up the bombers before reaching the target, which was Berlin, and escort them to the target and part of the way back home. Blue 1 and his wing man had to abort and I took over the flight. My second stage blower was out and I was having a little trouble keeping up since we were flying at about 23-24,000 feet. At a point about NW of Berlin, I observed a large formation of contrails climbing up at about 3 o'clock. They were under the sun, which was at about 2 or 3 o'clock at this time. We turned 90 degrees and started climbing so as to be above the formation that was climbing up to meet us. As they drew nearer I observed them to be FW 190s. While we were climbing, one formation of 190's came down diving slightly across my nose, going at 90 degrees to me. There were about 10 or 12 190's in this formation and they were flying in line abreast with the exception of one a/c in the center of the formation which was lagging behind about 300 yards. I turned in on the tail of the 190 and closed up to get into position to fire. Evidently I was unobserved as the e/a took no evasive action at all. I opened fire at about 300 yards at about a 5 degree angle off. I gave the e/a about one third of a Radius-Ring load and observed strikes on Right Wing, Right side of Fuselage and Engine. I gave about a two or three second burst. I observed a large piece of metal come off the right wing and the engine began to smoke. I opened fire again at about 150-200 yards with a line astern shot. I fired about a two second burst and one of my guns jammed. I observed strikes on fuselage and wing roots. Flame burst out of the right side of the engine. The e/a went over into a lazy spiral. The spiral got tighter as he went down. I broke back up to climb for position and altitude. This had taken place at approximately 20,000-25,000 feet at an I.A.S. of about 225-250 mph.

After climbing back for position and altitude, I noticed a formation of between 20 to 30 e/a climbing up South of us. These were reported almost at the same time by several pilots. At this time the formation of FW 190s was pretty well broken up. They appeared to have very little desire to stick around and mix it up with us. I got into position to attack the e/a which we observed to be Me 110s. I went down to attack the Me 110s with three or four more of my squadron. The Me 110s were flying close formation. I went in on the formation from 6 o'clock at about a 10 or 15 degree angle off. Before I started firing, I observed an Me 110 burst into flame on the opposite side of the formation. I do not know who shot this e/a down. I then opened fire on an Me 110 at about 350-400 yards, firing a two or three second burst. I observed strikes all around the cockpit area. I stopped firing and closed to about 200 yards. I opened fire again and closed to about 75 yards firing two 1 1/2 or 2 second bursts. I observed lots of strikes around wing root and cockpit area. A good many strikes were in the glasshouse (canopy). I'm fairly certain I must have killed the pilot. The e/a was smoking badly and went over into a spiral dive. At this point the clouds were fairly thin, being mostly haze. The pilot made no evident effort to get the a/c out of the dive. I watched the e/a down to what I thought was about 5,000 feet of he ground at which time it was still going straight down in a spiral and smoking badly. I am certain that this flame was beginning to come out of the right engine. The e/a could never have pulled out. As I was climbing back up, I observed another Me 110 diving slightly at about 9 o'clock to me. I went after the e/a, closed to about 400 yards and started firing. Another one of my guns had jammed by this time. I climbed to about 250 yards of the e/a and observed strikes on the left wing and engine nacelle. Before I could close up the e/a went into a cloud. I climbed back up and was joined by Lt. Millikan and noticed two FW 190s that were trying to come down on us. We started climbing into them. They broke down so we went after them. On the way down we saw a Me 110 diving away which Lt. Millikan had shot down. My wingman, Lt. Carlson, joined me at this time. Lt. Carlson developed engine trouble and the three of us started for home. He went down on the deck due to icing and engine trouble. When we came to the French coast, we crossed at the town of Bologne. My engine and Glycol was shot up by light flak. I pulled up to 700-800 feet and bailed out. I was taken prisoner immediately upon landing.

During the day's engagement I fired what I judge to be about 3/4 of my ammunition. I claim 1 FW 190 and 1 Me 110 destroyed and 1 Me 110 damaged.

I was Liberated on 1 May 1945 by the Russians and sent to "Lucky Strike" where a report of the above action was submitted.

s/ Vermont Garrison
t/ Vermont Garrison
0-886027
1st Lt., AC., Pilot

Ironically, the flak batteries that brought Lt. Garrison down were the last line of defenses that he would have to pass over before reaching the channel. Fate had dealt an unkind blow to both the squadron and the man who had just fought his most outstanding battle of World War II.

In the words of *Grover Hall, "The German flak gunners could congratulate themselves on having brought down one of the 4th's most gifted pilots. With **10 planes shot down, many bets were on him to win the Ace race."

Parachute-borne Lt. Garrison landed on a beach near Bologne. His capture was effected by members of a German anti-aircraft battery located near the coastline. Although he had suffered some injuries from flak fragments and hitting the rudder of his plane when he bailed out, Garry was immediately taken to an interrogation room for questioning and then confined to a bunker where he awaited transportation to a POW camp.

The following day he was put aboard a train to Germany, and upon arrival was taken to a Luftwaffe interrogation center for more questioning. During the two weeks that he was at this center, Garry was subjected to various forms of questioning and was surprised when the Germans produced his gun camera film during one of these sessions. This tactic, according to Hans Scharff, Germany's master interrogator, was designed to stun the prisoner and make him believe that there was nothing that they did not know about his background. Lt. Garrison refused to provide any information of intelligence value to his captors.

From the interrogation center, Garrison was sent to Stalag Luft I where he was quickly reunited with several of his friends from the 4th Fighter Group as well as a number of the 8th Fighter Command's more notable aviators, such as Francis "Gabby" Gabreski, "Hub" Zemke and Gerald "Jerry" Johnson of the 56th Fighter Group. Life in the camp was not easy. About 24 men were crowded into each barracks, and the main concerns each day were food and warmth. Some of the prisoners attempted to escape, but none succeeded. All of the prisoners in Garrison's barracks tried to make the best of a bad situation by maintaining their sense of humor, which left the Germans a bit flabbergasted.

Garrison shared an example of such humor: "As in all the camps, we were hit by periodic unannounced "shakedown" inspections. These usually occurred after 'lights out'. One of the favorite morale boosters was playing tricks on the guards. On one occasion we found out that we were going to be hit that evening and decided to have a little fun with the guards. Just prior to the time of inspection everyone took up various positions in the pitch dark barracks and waited. You can imagine the looks on their faces when they barged in, flipped on the lights, and found some of us playing cards, reading a book or writing a letter home. The startled Germans cut the inspection short, and we all got a good laugh. It was this type of humor that kept life going in the camp."

Liberation finally came on 1 May 1945 when the Russians overran the camp, and Vermont Garrison was among those who were airlifted to the American sector by B-17. Many of the former prisoners also went to "Camp Lucky Strike" and thence home, but Garry opted to return to his squadron in Debden and was provided transportation to do so.

Lt. Garrison's stay with the 336th FS was a short one, however, as the squadron was disbanded in September of 1945, and most of the personnel returned to the United States. Garrison, however, was assigned to the 406th Fighter Group and stayed in Europe as part of the Army of Occupation until 1946. His next assignment was to the 56th Fighter Group which was based at Selfridge Field, Michigan.

*Author of "1,000 Destroyed: The Life and Times of the 4th Fighter Group".
**Wartime claim. Grover Hall's assessment differs from the official record.

From 1947 to 1950 Garrison was assigned to Andrews Air Force Base, Maryland, as a member of the 4th Fighter Group. He was promoted to the rank of captain in 1947. While at Andrews, Garrison led the U.S. Air Force Acrobatic Team and also the winning team in the first "World-Wide Weapons Meet" which was held in Las Vegas, Nevada. During this tour he was also checked out in the F-80 and F-86 jets as they entered the Air Force inventory.

During the summer of 1950, Captain Garrison was transferred to Nellis Air Force Base, Nevada, to attend a gunnery course. In 1951 he was promoted to major and remained at Nellis as a gunnery instructor, research and development officer, and commander of the 3596th Advanced Applied Tactics Squadron. His responsibilities included the training of new and "retread" pilots in preparation for their deployment to combat assignments in Korea.

While Major Garrison was serving this tour of duty at Nellis, his old outfit was redesignated the 4th Fighter Interceptor Wing and sent to Japan where it was committed to the support of ground forces in Korea from Johnson Air Base. In the spring of 1951, the Wing was moved from Japan to Korea and operated from airfields in Suwan and Taegu until finally established at Kimpo during September. It was during these early days in Korea that the Wing Commander, Colonel J. K. Johnson, requested that Major Garrison be assigned to his command. This request was honored, and Major Vermont Garrison joined the 4th FIW in November of 1952 as Operations Officer of the 335th Fighter Interceptor Squadron which was equipped with F-86s. He served in this capacity until January 1953 when he assumed command of the squadron.

During his first month in command, Garrison flew seventeen missions without a successful encounter with an enemy aircraft. His luck changed on 21 February while leading a mission in "MiG Alley" when a flight of MiG 15s was spotted and quickly engaged in a classic "dog fight." Garrison was so intent upon maneuvering into a position to fire at his first target that he failed to see a MiG 15 rapidly closing on him. He missed the opportunity to fire on his intended victim by overshooting due to excessive speed. The pilot of the MiG opened fire as Garrison passed him, which caused Garry to do some violent, evasive maneuvering. Fortunately, the enemy fire missed his aircraft, and by now he had been rejoined by his wingman, who was after a second nearby MiG. The result was that the two MiG targets and two F-86 aggressors entered a large "Lufbery Circle" and stayed in it until the MiGs broke away. The MiG pilots paid dearly for this mistake. As they left the Lufbery, the two American pilots successfully took them under fire with the result that both Garrison and his wingman claimed the downing of one MiG each. The downing of Garry's first enemy jet aircraft had been a tough one, and this mission reminded him of the pilot's old addage to "Check Six" (Look for enemy to the rear.).

During the early part of March 1953 the communist pilots no longer displayed the aggressiveness they had during January and February, and the number of aerial encounters were significantly diminished. However, during the last ten days of March the MiGs again became quite active and ventured south in order to make a show of force over the front lines. As a result of this activity, the number of encounters increased dramatically as the 4th FIW was normally present to meet the enemy head on. On March 26th Major Garrison led a flight of four F-86s on a preemptive mission deep into enemy territory. As they arrived over the reservoir near Sui-ho, Garry spotted a flight of six MiGs crossing the Yalu River into Korea and immediately took them under attack. He chose his target, turned after it, and was quickly spotted by the pilot of his target who tried to escape by entering a series of diving and rolling maneuvers to get out of harm's way. The attempt was in vain, however, as Garry closed quickly and took the enemy aircraft under accurate fire which initially crippled the MiG. An additional burst blew off the canopy and caused the MiG to enter a spiral earthward, crashing and bursting into flame near the reservoir.

The air battles of late March resulted in the destruction of 34 enemy aircraft as opposed to two friendly losses. The impact and severity of these one-sided losses were evidently felt by the North Koreans as shown by the dearth of aerial encounters during the month of April. A few air battles were fought, however, and American pilots did make some claims. Major Garrison flew seventeen missions during April and claimed a "probable" on the 17th. The enemy also claimed some success during the month by downing two American "Aces." Captain Harold Fischer was shot down and taken prisoner, while Captain Joe McConnell was rescued and returned to duty.

May and June found the air war increasing in tempo as USAF pilots downed MiGs in record numbers. The enemy pilots encountered during this period were considered aggressive, but they lacked the skill of their predecessors. As a result, the "Ace Race" really took off. Garry Garrison returned to the scoring column in May by downing two MiG 15s, the first of which was credited for an encounter which occurred on the 17th during a mission deep into North Korea. As he and his wingman approached the Yalu River, Major Garrison spotted two enemy fighters and dove after them. The chase took the flight of two across the Yalu into Manchuria where they were taken under attack by a flight of six MiGs which separated Garrison from his wingman. Through a series of violent maneuvers, Garry was able to outfly his attackers. As the MiG pilots gave up the chase and broke away, he heard a distress call from a nearby F-86 pilot and rushed to his aid at a point near the mouth of the Yalu. Garry immediately took one of the tormentors under fire and with three quick bursts from his fifties ripped the enemy aircraft apart, which caused the pilot to eject. After evading damage from attack by an additional two MiGs, he heavily damaged a MiG before breaking off to escort the pilot of the crippled F-86 back to home base.

Garry's second downing during May came on the 23rd. While leading a flight of four F-86s on a mission over North Korea in the vicinity of Yonsu-dong, he spotted a flight of two MiGs and initiated the attack. He quickly pulled in at an angle behind his target and opened fire, raking the fuselage and tail section. The pilot ejected just before the tail section fell away and the aircraft exploded, giving Garrison credit for his fourth enemy aircraft destroyed in aerial combat in Korea.

June of 1953 was the banner month of Vermont Garrison's tour of duty with the 335th FIS. Although he only flew fifteen missions during the month, he made the most of his flying time by shooting down five enemy aircraft and damaging two others. His record began on 5 June when Garry was leading the squadron's Yellow Flight on a fighter sweep along the Yalu River. The other pilots in the formation were Captain Lonnie Moore, Lt. Harry Jones and Lt. Bill Schrimsher. The formation of F-86s was at 45,000 feet when Garrison saw dust traces from MiGs taking off from Feng Cheng Airfield. He turned north and led his flight across the Yalu to get into position for an attack. As they arrived over the field, they saw from 30 to 40 aircraft lined up and departing in take-off sequence. The flight peeled off and entered a steep dive in the direction of the airfield. As they passed through 20,000 feet, Garrison observed and ignored a gaggle of 15 to 20 MiGs orbiting the airfield to provide cover for the planes which were taking off and thus posed a serious threat to the safety of his formation.

Major Garrison leveled off at about 500 feet behind a formation of the low level MiGs and opened fire at the nearest one. His long and accurate burst caused his target to explode, and instead of taking evasive action Garrison flew through the life threatening debris so that the members of this flight could continue their targeting concentration. He quickly attacked a second MiG and riddled it with gunfire until it exploded. At this point the Major picked out a third target, but being low on ammunition, he switched places with his wingman, and Lt. Jones sent the MiG crashing. Moments later Captain Moore and Lt. Schrimisher each claimed a MiG, which brought Yellow Flight's total to five enemy aircraft destroyed during this mission, and rendered Major Garrison the 32nd aviator to attain "Ace" status in jet aircraft during the conflict. At age 37 he was also the oldest to claim this achievement.

The overhead flight of MiGs which was supposed to be providing cover for their comrades taking off, having obviously been taken by surprise at the sudden American onslaught, swooped downward after Garrison's flight only to be frustrated in their pursuit. Fortunately for the Americans, the Saber Jets had maintained most of their high diving speed and made a clean getaway. In less than two minutes, Garrison's flight had shot down more than half of the enemy formation which it attacked and caused the remainder to withdraw from action in defeat.

Vermont Garrison was promoted to Lt. Colonel shortly after this mission and remained in command of his squadron. His next combat exploit came on 24 June during a fighter sweep in North Korea. As he was nearing the Yalu River, he observed four MiGs preparing to attack a flight of Sabre Jets and immediately maneuvered to take them under fire. Closing rapidly on the leader, he opened fire at long range and scored telling hits, which caused the enemy pilot to make a series of evasive turns. Garrison pressed the attack, and his accurate machine gun fire caused the MiG to burst into flame as the pilot ejected. The remainder of the enemy flight broke off the engagement and fled to safety across the Yalu.

On 26 June, while Colonel Garrison and his wingman were on combat air patrol, he sighted a formation of eight MiGs at low level apparently using a thin cloud layer for cover. As he initiated a high speed diving attack, six of the enemy aircraft broke away in a desperate attempt to reach safety north of the Yalu. Garrison cut off one of the two remaining MiGs and, despite a series of violent evasive maneuvers, skillfully gained a position from which his well aimed guns raked the enemy's fuselage, causing the MiG to roll over and crash, exploding as it hit the ground. This was Garrison's eighth confirmed enemy aircraft destroyed.

His ninth downing came on 30 June while Garry was leading a flight of four Sabre Jets on fighter patrol deep in North Korea. When nearing the Sui-Ho Reservoir, he saw a large force of MiG 15s at a lower altitude and led his flight in a high speed attack, selecting the last aircraft of the formation as his target. His first burst of fire hit the MiG and caused the enemy pilot to turn violently in an effort to avoid further damage. Garry employed the maximum of performance from his aircraft in retaining the offensive and maneuvering into firing position. His next burst caught the MiG in the engine section and caused it to explode and disintegrate. The remainder of the MiGs fled across the Yalu.

Early July was a period marked by heavy rains which kept the fighters of both sides grounded until the 10th. As the weather improved the incidence of aerial encounters rose, and the Americans noted that they were engaging better enemy pilots than they had during May and June. Lt. Colonel Garrison shot down his tenth MiG on Sunday the 19th while leading a fighter sweep along the Yalu. Upon spotting a flight of MiGs, he immediately attacked the formation and selected his target. Garry's first burst of fire hit the engine, which emitted a heavy cloud of smoke. His second well placed burst ripped the fuselage open and loosed a sheet of flame from within.

The MiG went into a spiral and the pilot was seen to eject before the plane crashed in a field. The Sabre pilots inflicted significant losses to the enemy during the month by destroying 32 MiGs against the loss of two F-86s.

Hamilton Air Force Base, California. (l to r): Senator Barry Goldwater, Lieutenant Colonel Harrison Ward, and Colonel Vermont Garrison, Base Commander, 1972. Source: Garrison Collection.

Vermont Garrison completed his tour of duty in Korea on 28 October 1953. His record of 10 enemy aircraft destroyed in aerial combat in Korea placed him in two select categories, the first of which is that only ten American aviators were credited with the destruction of 10 or more enemy aircraft during the Korean Conflict. The second is that he became one of but seven aviators eligible for inclusion in this book by becoming an "Ace" during World War II in piston driven aircraft and again an "Ace" in jet propelled fighters in Korea. It should also be noted that in just seven months of combat flying in Korea the "The Kentucky Marksman" not only destroyed ten enemy aircraft but was also credited with an additional 4 "Probables" and 5 "Damaged."

After a well earned leave, Garry began his assignment with the 4750th Training Wing at Vincent AFB, Arizona, where he remained until being sent to the Marine Corps Senior Officers School in 1957. During the three years after graduation in 1958 Garrison served in the Pentagon and then at Tyndall AFB. He was promoted to Colonel in March of 1961 and sent to Spokane, Washington, where he served as an advisor to the Washington Air National Guard and later joined the staff of the 25th Air Division at McChord AFB.

Colonel Garrison was transferred from McChord to the Far East for a tour of duty with the 405th Fighter Wing. His initial assignment was as Director of Operations, and in August 1965 he became Deputy Commander of the Wing. He was named Commander of the 405th in January 1966 and remained in this position until he was assigned to Ubon, Thailand, to serve as Vice Commander of the 8th Tactical Fighter Wing. A summary of his exploits and personal qualities is best provided by BG (Retired) Robin Olds:

"Garry was my Vice Wing CO of the 8th TFW at Ubon, Thailand, in '66, early '67. Known by the younger pilots as "The Grey Eagle, ` Garry flew his 52nd SEA mission on his 52nd birthday. To my mind that beats hell out of shootii g your age in golf!

64

"The old character wheedled his way into the 8th prior to my arrival as CO and never bothered to tell anyone that he really wasn't checked out in the F-4. He was smart enough always to fly with an IP in the back seat—but that youngster was for knob and switch advice only. Once airborne and over the target, no one dropped 'em cleaner or more accurately than old "Vermouth" or Garry (whichever you prefer). That is except one day when he dropped his glasses, couldn't retrieve them before roll-in, and was lucky to hit the country of Laos!

"Of the many hundreds I've served with Garry was one of the greatest—as pilot, as gentleman, as officer, and as friend."

During this tour of duty in his third war, Colonel Garrison flew 97 missions in the F-4 Phantom. He and Robin Olds certainly proved Defense Secretary MacNamera wrong when the Secretary stated to reporters, "There are no 'grandfathers' flying as fighter pilots in Vietnam." General Olds, an "Ace" in WW II, destroyed 4 MiGs while commanding the 8th TFW.

Colonel Garrison completed this assignment on 5 June 1967 and returned to the United States to become Commanding Officer of the 408th Fighter Group at Kingsley Field, Oregon, where he remained until being transferred to Perrin Field, Texas, in 1969 as Wing Commander. Garrison closed out his 32 year career at Hamilton Field, California, where he served as Commander of the 4661st Air Base Group from 1971 until his retirement on 1 March 1973.

Although adequately reflected by the medals Vermont Garrison was awarded for heroism well above and beyond the call of duty, and for superior airmanship, combat leadership and service, it is clear that Colonel Garrison was a rare, true American patriot and fighting man.

After retirement Vermont Garrison settled down in Idaho and kept himself busy by hunting, fishing, and traveling until he succumbed to a heart attack on 14 February 1994. It is certain that the legend of "The Kentucky Marksman" will be revered in the annals of aviation history and continue to serve as a model for aspiring combat aviators over the years which lie ahead.

Colonel Vermont Garrison
United States Air Force, Retired
SN 0-886027 & 0-33987a

Awards and Decorations
Distinguished Service Cross
Silver Star with One Oak Leaf Cluster
Legion Of Merit with One Oak Leaf Cluster
Distinguished Flying Cross with Six Oak Leaf Clusters
Bronze Star Medal with Two Oak Leaf Clusters
Purple Heart Medal
Air Medal with Ten Oak Leaf Clusters
USAF Commendation Medal

Service Medals
American Defense Service Medal
American Campaign Medal
European-African-Middle East Campaign Medal
World War II Victory Medal
Army Of Occupation Medal (Germany)
National Defense Service Medal
Korean Service Medal
Air Force Longevity Service Award with Four Oak Leaf Clusters

Foreign Service Awards
United Nations Service Medal

Credits For Enemy Aircraft Destroyed During Combat Actions

Date		Aircraft Destroyed	Mission	Location
	World War II			
1943	16 December	.333 Ju- 88	Escort	Zuider Zee
1944	14 January	2 FW 190	Fighter Sweep	Compeigne Woods
	31 January	1 Me 109	Escort	Gilze-Rijen
	6 February	1 FW 190	Escort	Beauvais-Margny
	10 February	1 Me 109	Escort	Dummer Lake
	25 February	1 FW 190	Escort	Luxembourg
	3 March	1 FW 190	Escort	Berlin
	Korea			
1953	21 February	1 MiG 15	Interceptor	Tangmok-tang
	26 March	1 MiG 15	Interceptor	Ta Sui Ho Reservoir
	17 May	1 MiG 15	Interceptor	Ta Yalu River
	23 May	1 MiG 15	Interceptor	Ta Yonsu-dong
	5 June	2 MiG 15	Fighter Sweep	Sui Ho, Namsan-Ni
	24 June	1 MiG 15	Fighter Sweep	Sakchu
	26 June	1 MiG 15	Combat Patrol	Namsi-dong
	30 June	1 MiG 15	Combat Patrol	Unbong-dong
	19 July	1 MiG 15	Fighter Sweep	Ch'oryon-gwan

SUMMARY: Colonel Garrison served in three conflicts with distinction. His legacy is of great importance to those who knew him and will serve as a positive example for those who follow.

Official Record: 17.333 Enemy Aircraft Destroyed, 3 Probably Destroyed, 8 Damaged, and .25 Destroyed on the ground.

Across: Lieutenant Colonel Vermont Garrison at Kimpo Air Force Base (K-14), Korea, Circa 1953.

Major James P. Hagerstrom in Korea, Circa 1952. Source: USAF File Photo

Chapter 5

Colonel James P. Hagerstrom

James Philo Hagerstrom was born in Cedar Falls, Iowa, on 14 January 1921, the third son of Mr. and Mrs. Edward R. Hagerstrom. His grandfather was a Swedish emigrant who departed the small town of Borlange, about 120 miles northwest of Stockholm, many years earlier in search of a better life in America.

When "Jim" was five years old, he had the opportunity to sit in the cockpit of a World War I vintage "Jenny" aircraft and was greatly impressed. In 1934, at age 13, Jim Hagerstrom had the thrill of his young life when he was treated to a fifty-cent, "once around the field" flight in a Ford tri-motor airplane. He had felt particularly good sitting in the wicker seats and enjoying the sights and sensations of this experience, which evidently left him with a lasting, positive impression of aerial flight.

While attending West High School in Waterloo, Iowa, he was a good student; he lettered in wrestling and graduated in January of 1939. Jim went on to attend Iowa State Teachers College, which was near the University of Iowa and a source of flight training. He underwent the necessary ground schooling and received about 35 hours of flight experience while keeping up with his college studies. However, Jim had flying on his mind, and on 6 December 1941 he traveled to Iowa City to meet with the Army Air Force Flying Cadet recruiter. After the initial interview he filled out a lot of forms, underwent a physical examination, and anxiously awaited the outcome.

The wait was not a long one, as he received orders during the first week of January 1942 directing him to report to Fort Des Moines for induction. On 15 January he was sworn into the U.S. Army Air Force and boarded a train to Bakersfield, California, where the group of new inductees was met at the station and transported to nearby Minter Field by military trucks. More paperwork and physicals occupied the next few days, and on 23 January his group was taken to Visalia, north of Bakersfield, to begin Primary Training.

Standard uniforms were not available for issue to the new cadets, and their initial month of training in the PT-22 airplane found them clad in coveralls. Most of the class members had undergone flight training prior to enlistment, and this was capitalized upon through an accelerated program. After graduation, in new uniforms, the class was transported to Minter Field, where Basic Flight Training was accomplished in the BT-13 aircraft. Coincidentally, Jim's older brother, Robert, was also undergoing Basic at that time, and they were able to be together for about six weeks. After graduation from this phase of training, the class proceeded to Luke Field, near Phoenix, Arizona, for Advanced Flight Training in the AT-6. One of Jim's classmates in this phase was Cotesworh Head, Jr., who went on to receive credit for downing 13 Japanese aircraft in the Southwest Pacific.

James P. Hagerstrom was commissioned a Second Lieutenant in the U.S. Army Reserve and also presented the coveted aviator "Wings" by Brigadier General Ennis C. Whitehead during the graduation ceremonies conducted on 26 July 1942. He was concurrently ordered to active duty with the U.S. Army Air Force and assigned to the 20th Pursuit Group. He flew P-39s and P-40s at both Myrtle Beach Air Base, South Carolina, and Pinnelas City Air Base, Florida. During the months of July and August, Jim was fortunate to record about 70 hours of flight time each month.

In late September a large number of lieutenants received orders for the 8th Fighter Squadron of the 5th Air Force's 49th Fighter Group, Pacific Theater of Operations. Their orders directed the aviators to travel by train to San Francisco, California, the first leg of the long journey which lay ahead. For this trip, and until such time as they would reach a firm destination, 2nd Lt. Hagerstrom was unofficially appointed "Quarters Officer," with very little to do while the group was aboard the train. After arrival in San Francisco, Lt. Hagerstrom asked the first civilian he saw, "Where is there a good hotel in this town?" The civilian answered, "Try the Mark Hopkins". Jim said, "OK, thanks!" he located the nearest phone and called the Mark Hopkins Hotel. He told the hotel operator that he would like to be connected to the manager. When the manager answered, Jim said, "We've got a problem. We have forty Second Lieutenants here on our way overseas and need a place to stay." There was silence on the phone for a moment and then the manager said, "Lieutenant, you guys just come over here." The forty pilots walked into the hotel lobby, overseas gear and all, and the manager charged each of them $5.00 per night for the individual suites he provided the entire group.

Fort Mason, California, was the next destination. After overseas processing, the group of young pilots was boarded on the Oslo-based Norwegian ship S.S. *Torance,* which passed under the Golden Gate Bridge on the way to the war zone in the Pacific the evening of the same day they had clambered aboard and been assigned their berths. Hagerstrom reflected that it had only been about ten months from his induction into the Air Force to date of this sailing.

After dark on the evening of departure, the *Torance* began a zig-zag course to Honolulu. On board was the entire staff of the 5th Air Force Headquarters along with the main force which was to man the organizations under its command—some 1,500 officers and enlisted men. The meals consisted of powdered eggs, toast, and coffee for breakfast; sardines and crackers for lunch, and beef and potatoes for supper during the few days it took to reach Hawaii. Upon arrival the officers were provided quarters at Hickam Field. While there, Hagerstrom and some of his friends pooled their funds and bought cases of canned food to supplement their shipboard diet in anticipation of a long trip to the combat zone.

The stay in Hawaii did not last long. The S.S. *Torance* was again boarded during the day, with departure taking place after dark on a zig-zag course westward. Upon arising the next morning the passengers were surprised to find their ship in the middle of a huge Naval Task Force, with the *Torance* between two battleships. From this point on there was no more zig-zagging, just smooth sailing until the end of October when the *Torence* broke out of the formation and, with a destroyer escort, headed toward the Fiji Islands. The port of Suva was used for an overnight stop, and both ships departed for Australia in the early morning hours.

About halfway there, the destroyer was relieved by an Australian Corvette, and it was learned that their destination was the port of Townsville. There was no one to meet the American contingent upon its arrival, and the only place which could be found to house the members of the 5th AF was some vacant barracks at a Royal Australian Air Force (RAAF) facility by the name of Garbut Field. It wasn't long until many thought they had been sent to war, but couldn't find it. Matters finally got straightened out and Brigadier General Paul "Squeeze" Wurtsmith, Commander of the 5th Air Force Fighter Command, set up a refresher training course for the young fighter pilots in his command. The next stop was Charters-Towers Field where they were joined by some experienced combat pilots who provided the rudiments of combat flying in P-38 and P-40 fighters.

Work on the preparation of an airstrip at Dobodura (about 15 miles from Bunda) had started in early November of 1942. The P-40 equipped 8th Fighter Squadron to which Lt. Hagerstrom was assigned had been located at a strip called "Three Mile" at Kila, New Guinea, and joined up with the rest of the 49th Fighter Group at Dobodura in early April of 1943. Hagerstrom had flown several missions while in New Guinea without incident. His promotion to First Lieutenant was received shortly after the 8th FS arrived at Dobodua. The

49th was composed of one P-38 and two P-40 Squadrons. As a matter of interest, a few of the P-38 pilots who would earn honors while with the 49th were Richard Bong, Gerald Johnson, and Bob DeHaven.

On 11 April, during a squadron mission, Lt. Hagerstrom experienced his first combat engagement while flying wingman to Captain Lawrence "Killer" Kirsch, who was purported to be "the fastest man from the sack to the cockpit of an airplane!" Shortly after take off Kirsch and Hagerstrom climbed to about 10,000 feet, and Jim could see fires in the water near Oro bay, evidently the remaining signs of aircraft which had been shot down. At a range of about five miles, he saw a group of aircraft engaged in aerial combat. Kirsch and Hagerstrom climbed to gain the advantage of a higher altitude prior to joining the fight. Their attacking dive took them through a Japanese formation and resulted in Kirsch acquiring a Zero on his tail. Hagerstrom immediately maneuvered to get behind the Zero where his first attempt to fire met dead silence as his gun switch was still in the "off" position. Before he could arm the guns and pursue his target he spotted the tail of a Zero on one side of his aircraft and the nose of a second one on his other side. He quickly rolled into a dive, turned on his arming switch and pulled out of the dive to join up with a nearby P-40 which turned out to be his leader, Kirsch. After a short skirmish Jim again became separated from his flight leader but spotted what he thought was a P-40 flying behind two P-38s and increased his airspeed to join them. The trailing plane turned out to be a Zero closing in on the P-38s and quickly became Jim's target. As Hagerstrom maneuvered into firing position, the Zero turned to the right, and from a distance of about 500 feet, Jim gave him a long burst which caused the plane to explode and fall into the ocean. His next move was to join up with a nearby P-40 which, again, turned out to be Captain Kirsch. At this point they headed for their home strip and landed with very little fuel remaining. The combat activity had lasted about an hour, and Kirsch was also credited with the destruction of a Zero during this mission.

During most of the spring and summer of 1943, the 8th FS flew escort missions for formations of C-47 transports which were dropping supplies to the land forces to support their combat operations and progress in the jungle. In the early fall the entire 49th FG was relocated to Tsilli Tsilli, New Guinea. The new operating base was a grass air strip in an area which had been occupied by Japanese forces until about two weeks before the Group's arrival. The extent to which the area had been cleared of enemy units and individuals by the fast moving American Forces was unknown, and it was thus necessary for all Air Force personnel to be armed and alert at all times. This uneasiness was added to by the almost nightly bombing of the airstrip, which became part of the routine. The standard protective slit trenches were innovatively dug by the pilots inside their living tents. They could be reached in split seconds, and were dry when needed.

Most of the 8th FS missions from the new airfield were to escort the B-25 and A-20 formations which were making low level attacks on targets located on Wewak Island. It was somewhat amazing that several Japanese aircraft were destroyed on the ground during each of these missions. The 8th FS experienced very little air to air combat during this period of operations, but activity increased when the squadron orientation was switched to protection of the high flying B-17 and B-24 bombers. There was, however, a slight impediment to the overall aggressiveness of the 8th FS. Tsilli Tsilli was at the end of a long supply line. Aircraft fuel, among the other supplies needed by the 49th and its units, had to be delivered by C-47s. There were days when pilots took off on missions without full fuel tanks, which reduced their combat effectiveness.

During an afternoon briefing session on 5 October, it was learned that a Japanese reconnaissance aircraft was flying over Finchhafen, and instructions were immediately given to intercept and shoot down the intruder. Eight aircraft from the 8th FS were quickly dispatched on this mission with Jim Hagerstrom leading a flight of four of them. At an altitude of 10,000 feet while approaching Finchafen, a twin engine Japanese "Dina" reconnaissance plane was spotted emerging from the clouds at a greater altitude than the American formation. Hagerstrom quickly switched fuel tanks, released his drop tank, and initiated a full throttle climb in the attack. As soon as the enemy saw the approaching fighters, he turned and accelerated to the point that black smoke was seen coming out of his tailpipes in an attempt to escape. The leader of the second flight of four informed Jim that he was going to take his flight back to home base on the basis that it did not take eight fighters to shoot down one unarmed plane. Shortly thereafter, Jim's number 3 and 4 pilots radioed that it didn't look as though the enemy could be overtaken and requested permission to discontinue the mission and return to home base, which Hagerstrom granted. As the pursuit continued Jim's wingman reported a rough engine and was instructed to return to Tsilli Tsilli.

Lt. Hagerstrom maintained his determined quest; at about 18,000 feet he was able to place fire on the right engine of the Dina and then quickly maneuvered into position to fire on the left one. The right engine exploded as he was firing on the left, and the Dina rolled before entering a vertical dive from which it did not recover. Jim followed the stricken plane down, using his gun camera to record the event and the huge explosion which resulted when the plane hit the water. It was about sundown at this time, Lt. Hagerstrom, alone, was very close to the Japanese air base at Madang. He stayed on the deck for protection during the nearly one hour flight back to his home base. Jim soon found that his navigational aids had become inoperative but knew that if he flew over Lae, which was still held by the Japanese, he would intercept the Markhar River and then the tributary which led to Tsilli Tsilli. His pass over Lae was so low and fast that he took the Japanese by surprise and not a shot was fired at him.

Hagerstrom reached Tsilli Tsilli after dark and radioed the tower to have the runway lights turned on so he could land. The reply was, "Unable. Japanese reconnaissance aircraft overhead." Short on fuel, and with no other choice, he lowered flaps and landing gear and approached what he thought should be the landing strip. Fortunately, his estimate was correct, and the landing was a safe one—on the strip. A dimly lighted "Follow Me" jeep led him to his parking area and the successful completion of a mission which resulted in credit for his second downed enemy aircraft.

Heavy rains arrived in late October and rapidly turned the airstrip into a quagmire. The P-38 squadrons were unable to operate as their nose wheels plowed the mud and prevented the aircraft from reaching the speed necessary to "rotate" the nose to a take-off attitude. It was thus left to the P-40 squadron to carry the entire Group mission load during this period. When the weather did let up a little, and the runway became a bit firmer, the P-38 squadrons were moved to a firmer airfield. The P-40 equipped 8th FS was relocated some 60 miles to the north of Tsilli Tsilli, about 50 miles northwest of Lae, to an airstrip by the name of "Gusap." Most of the missions from the new base were in the role of escort for bombers whose target was Wewak, about 240 miles to the north of Gusap. Lt. Hagerstrom contracted malaria during this period and was evacuated to Australia for treatment and recuperation which took three weeks.

Upon his return to the 8th FS, Lt. Hagerstrom resumed normal duty with no apparent aftereffects from his illness. During January of 1944, Lt. Hagerstrom flew 36 missions in just eighteen days, with the most memorable and significant of WW II being the B-24 escort mission flown on 23 January. On this day Jim was leading a flight of P-40s with 2nd Lt. John Bodak as his wingman. As the combined formation was proceeding to the target area, the pilots of number three and four aircraft reported malfunctions and returned to

Gusap. The remaining two aircraft then took up positions above and to the rear of the B-24s to try to capitalize their effectiveness at about 25,000 feet. There were also formations of P-38s and P-47s providing protective cover for the bombers at a greater altitude.

Just as the B-24s were unleashing their bomb loads on Wewak, a P-38 pilot reported Zeros coming in high. Jim and his wingman fell back a bit in order to obtain a better view of the overall scene and dropped their auxiliary tanks in preparation for the certain fight ahead. They spotted descending P-38s as well as the attacking Zeros, all of which passed downward through their altitude at high speed. The two P-40s rolled and dived, joining the engagement at about 15,000 feet. As he pulled up, Jim had a Zero in his sights and quickly fired, scoring hits in the wing root area with no observable results. He was closing so fast that he passed under the tail of the Zero and then descended almost to the deck where there were several more enemy planes milling around just off the shore of the targeted Wewak. In rapid succession Jim shot down a Hamp as the result of a head-on firing pass, followed by another Hamp and then one more Hamp. While he was turning back to the main grouping of enemy aircraft, he picked up a Tony right in front of him at about 400 yards and gave him a long burst which caused the plane to come apart and to plunge into the water, bringing his credits to four downed aircraft for the day. Hagerstrom and his wingman remained in the fight and went on to severely damage three more Zeros before returning to their distant home base. Official records credited Hagerstrom with one Tony and three Hamps on this date. The "Hamp" was an improved version of the Zero.

The squadron celebrated a highly successful day of combat upon the return of all aircraft to Gusap. The festivities centered around Lt. Jim Hagerstrom who had shot down four of the six enemy aircraft claimed by the 8th FS during this important and decisive series of encounters. The event also celebrated Jim's elevation to the status of "Ace" among his peers. Additionally, the 23rd of January marked the last day that Lt. Hagerstrom was to shoot down an adversary during WW II.

Early February found Lt. Hagerstrom with orders to return to the United States after completion of 170 missions in the South Pacific. His leave period in Iowa was met with snow and cold weather, a far cry from the heat and humidity of the tropical islands. After a well deserved rest and reunion with his family, he reported to the Reassignment Center in Miami, Florida. His request for assignment to an organization equipped with jet aircraft was ignored as no one at the center had heard of such an aircraft or unit. His immediate destination turned out to be as an Instructor of Applied Tactics in P-47s at an air base located near Orlando, Florida.

During this assignment he became acquainted with a WASP (Women's Auxiliary Service Pilot) named Virginia "Lee" Jowell. The whirlwind courtship which ensued culminated in their marriage on 25 July 1944. Shortly thereafter, Lee was transferred to Brownsville, Texas, for training and qualification in fighter aircraft. One month later Jim was moved to Evansville, Indiana, where he became an Air Corps test pilot at the Republic Aviation plant which was producing forty-seven P-47s per day at that time. Upon completion of her training in fighter aircraft, Lee was assigned to Evansville as a ferry pilot for the delivery of new P-47s to continental air bases and airfields near ports of embarkation where the Thunderbolts were prepared for overseas shipment. She was thus able to rejoin her husband after a relatively short separation. Although they were not always at home at the same time, this arrangement was far better than serving in distant, individual assignments.

Jim Hagerstrom was promoted to Captain in January of 1945. His duty station remained Evansville until 6 September, when he was separated from the Air Force. He and his young bride, now pregnant and no longer a WASP, returned to Waterloo, Iowa, where Jim immediately enrolled in Teachers College. In the fall he transferred to the University of Iowa and in October their first of eight children, Michelle, was born. Jim received a Bachelor of Arts Degree in economics during the graduation ceremonies conducted in June of 1946.

The Hagerstrom family moved to Houston, Texas, where Jim was employed in an investment securities firm which was owned by Mr. A. W. Snyder. Snyder was a West Point graduate and military pilot who had flown in both WW I and WW II. The work and relationship went well, but within six months of embarking on this career Jim's desire to fly surfaced and he joined a nearby Air Force Reserve unit. It was necessary for him to go through the formality of being checked out in the unit's AT-6 aircraft, during which he asked his instructor how he could find a way to fly the P-51s which were located on the other side of the airfield they were using. He was advised that they belonged to the National Guard.

Whether by coincidence, perception or something which had been dropped in conversation, the following day Jim's boss asked him, "Would you like to join the National Guard and fly the P-51s?" The answer was a definite, "Yes," and Mr. Snyder then picked up the phone and called the National Guard unit commander. He said, "Colonel, I have a young man in my office who has 1,200 hours of flying time with 170 missions and six Japanese aircraft to his credit. He would like to join the National Guard." When the conversation ended Mr. Snyder said, "You go to the National Guard this Saturday and join up." Captain Hagerstrom thus obtained release from the Army Reserve and joined the 111th Fighter Squadron of the Texas Air National Guard, got checked out in the P-51, and within 6 months was the Squadron Operations Officer.

It should be noted that keeping a sharp gunnery eye was a major element of Hagerstrom's training program. In the course of time and events, Jim met a Mr. J. D. Reed who somehow had acquired and was refitting a P-51D for the Cleveland Air Races. Jim flew to the races expecting to fly the P-51 only to find that the plane had been sold to Jacqueline "Jackie" Cochran, the lady of aviation fame, who in turn sold it to Bill Odom. Jim took the time to check Odom out in this particular P-51 so that he could use the aircraft for racing and other purposes; however, Odom was killed in a tragic accident on 6 September 1949. It was learned that J. D. Reed also owned a P-38, which was located in New Orleans, and had installed two new engines on the plane in preparation for the 1949 races in Cleveland. As it turned out, Jim Hagerstrom flew both the P-38 and P-51 in the 1949 Cleveland Air Races, an excellent example of perseverance in the quest of a goal.

Jim was promoted to Major in June of 1950 and was designated commander of the 111th FS. Upon the outbreak of hostilities in Korea that month, the 111th FS was federalized, assigned to the Tactical Air Command (TAC), and transferred to Langley Air Force Base in Virginia. Shortly thereafter, Major Hagerstrom was assigned to TAC Headquarters, and during this assignment was checked out in the new T-33 and F-80 aircraft. He also was able to convince the Deputy Commander for Operations that TAC should send some of the pilots occupying staff jobs to Korea to fly a combat tour in F-86s, and in August of 1952 Major Hagerstrom was sent to Nellis Air Force Base to attend F-80 and F-86 Gunnery School. Hagerstrom's instructor at Nellis was Captain William T. Whisner, also a member of "The Inner Seven." Upon completion of gunnery training, Jim was transferred to Korea via San Francisco and Japan with full anticipation of successfully completing 100 combat missions in the F-86. His assignment upon reaching the combat zone was to the 334th Fighter Interceptor Squadron (FIS) of the 4th Fighter Interceptor Wing (FIW).

During one of his early missions on 21 November 1952, Hagerstrom was flying as wingman to Major Bernie Bailey. As they were returning to their base, and about 100 miles south of the Yalu, they spotted two MiG 15s at different altitudes. It was decided that Jim would take the lower one and Bailey the higher, and the attack began. Jim slid in behind his target and gave it a long and accurate burst of fire from his guns. The enemy pilot bailed out, and a few seconds later the aircraft exploded. The post-mission inspection of his aircraft at Kimpo Air Base (K-14) revealed that a piece of the MiG was embedded in the wing of Hagerstrom's F-86.

One of the squadron pilots had planned to be Santa Claus at a local orphanages on Christmas Day, and when he found that he was scheduled to be on "alert" that day, asked Jim to take his place, which he did. The alert pilots were called out, quickly took off, and intercepted a flight of 6 MiGs just south of the Yalu River at about 36,000 feet. Hagerstrom was flying in the number 3 position of the formation and was advised to get behind two of the targeted MiGs. As he did so, one of them broke away which left Jim behind the leader of that section at a distance of about 1,000 feet. The pilot of the MiG rolled over and Hagerstrom followed suit, acquiring a clear shot as he was looking down on the cockpit of the enemy plane. The MiG entered a vertical dive, and the pilot bailed out. Jim rejoined his formation to find that the fight was over and the flight was headed for Kimpo with Major Hagerstrom having recorded the downing of his second enemy aircraft over Korea.

January of 1953 found Major Hagerstrom transferred to the 18th Fighter Bomber Wing (FBW) at Osan (K-55) to take charge of the conversion of the wing from propeller driven P-51s to the jet powered F-86s. Upon his arrival, he determined that receipt of the F-86s was still some time in the future and, per his request, was allowed to return to the 4th FIW to continue flying combat missions. By mid-January, however, the delivery schedule had been advanced, and he returned to Osan with the task of organizing and overseeing the transition of the wing's 125 P-51 pilots into the F-86. Three squadrons were involved with this conversion. Then it was a period of bitter winter weather, and there were not many instructor pilots available to assist with this demanding effort. Despite the impediments, the task was completed in 30 days with no mishaps.

On 25 February, as Jim was leading a flight with Major Harry Evans as his wingman, he located a flight of three MiGs. The enemy pilots quickly spotted the approaching Sabre Jets and ducked into a layer of clouds trailing black smoke, the sign of over-acceleration. The sun was behind the two Sabres as they followed the smoke through the clouds, and when they reached clear air, they found the enemy aircraft directly in front of them along with another layer of clouds. During this time, Colonel Royal Baker, the formation leader, was trying to contact Hagerstrom in an effort to find out where the MiGs were. As Jim was busy stalking his prey he radioed, "Hold on Colonel," and Baker then repeated his query. At this point, Hagerstrom radioed Baker, "I'm at the headwaters of the Mizu." (Mizu means water in Japanese.) Actually, Jim and his wingman were over a tributary of the Yalu. River.

As Jim and his wingman broke through the next cloud layer, they could not find the two MiGs they were pursuing but spotted a MiG which was firing on a nearby Sabre Jet. Hagerstrom immediately took the MiG under fire, causing the enemy pilot to break off his attack and enter a dive. Jim got on his tail and stayed there until they were on the deck, so low that they were flying below the tops of the brick industrial smoke stacks of Mukden— —China. The MiG pilot's violent maneuvering made the placement of fatal machine gun bursts difficult but not impossible. By the time the enemy pilot released his canopy and bailed out, Major Hagerstrom had already identified another nearby target which began a climb, closely followed by the Americans. At this point, Jim was 100 miles north of the Yalu and running low on fuel. Several MiGs were spotted at various altitudes heading north, presumably to find out what Sabres were doing in the Mukden area. The climb took them through several cloud layers and caused them to lose sight of their immediate prey. They leveled off at 52,000 feet and headed for home. With two airfields between their position and home base of Osan, they were not overly concerned about running out of fuel and decided to stretch their decent and both landed safely. However, Hagerstrom had just enough fuel to make it to a parking revetment, and his wingman ran out while still on the runway. The action resulted in Major Hagerstrom being awarded credit for the downing of his third MiG.

The mission of 13 March involved the entire squadron and found Major Hagerstrom leading a flight of four Sabres, with Captain Elmer Dunlap as his wingman, positioned above the rest of the formation. About 70 miles south of the Yalu, the pilots of his numbers 3 and 4 aircraft reported mechanical problems and were ordered to return to Osan. At about the same time Jim spotted two MiGs, signaled his wingman to drop the auxiliary fuel tanks, and commenced the attack. He reported this action by a radio transmission to the squadron commander stating, "Colonel, going to leave you for a while, got a couple of MIGs up here." Jim opened fire from a position to the rear of the enemy planes, and after a long burst his target started to come apart and then exploded right in front of him. The remaining pilot then attacked Hagerstrom, and after a few quick maneuvers Jim got behind the MiG, which had begun to climb and head north. They passed the Yalu at about 48,000 feet, and Jim continued his intermittent bursts of fire with no obvious results. He finally took up a position very close to the rear of the MiG and fired until he ran out of ammunition, at which time he pulled alongside his adversary to determine its condition. He found that the flaps were actually "flapping," there was liquid flowing out of the engine area, and the engine was dead. By this time they were over a large airfield, "About the size of Barksdale AFB", according to Hagerstrom, which turned out to be Antung——one of the largest in Manchuria—— located half way between Mukden and Port Arthur. Jim instructed his wingman to "finish off" the MiG and observed the enemy pilot bail out right over what was presumed to be his home airfield. Major Hagerstrom received credit for the downing of one and one half enemy aircraft, and his wingman was credited for the other half. With a total of four and one half aircraft destroyed in the air, Jim was now very close to being declared a "Jet Ace."

The daily missions continued but were unproductive for Hagerstrom until 27 March when, flying just south of the Yalu River, the flight which he was leading flew right through a formation of four MiGs, amazingly with not a shot being fired by any of the opponents. It can only be concluded that restricted visibility thwarted the possibility of a combat engagement. A few minutes later, dead ahead and at a lower altitude, Major Hagerstrom located six MiGs which were in no semblance of a formation—— "scattered" was the term he used to describe what he observed. He initiated an attack dive from the rear and instructed his wingman to, "Pick out a MiG, but don't fire until I say go." As Jim pulled in behind one of the MiGs, he saw the airplane's wing drop, figured that the pilot was going to look behind him and ordered, "Go!" Jim opened fire on his target and the initial burst shot off his adversary's wing tip without seriously impeding the MiG's flyability. After a series of diving and climbing maneuvers, during which Hagerstrom was firing short bursts, he attained an advantageous position from which he fired a long and accurate stream of bullets. Moments later the MiG pilot bailed out, and the plane spiraled and crashed on the enemy airfield which was directly below the action. The flight of two then headed for their home base, but while enroute they came upon a stray MiG which Major Hagerstrom took under fire and easily shot out of the sky. Hagerstrom now had credit for the downing of 6 1/2 enemy aircraft, had attained "Jet Ace" status, and became the 28th "Ace" of the Korean Conflict and the fifth member of "The Inner Seven." It should also be noted that he was the only member of the 18th Fighter Bomber Wing to attain "Ace" status.

His next encounter took place on 13 April while Major Hagerstrom was on a mission over North Korea. At 49,000 feet he located a single MiG and moved into an excellent attack position from which he fired a long and deadly burst, causing parts to fly off of his target. The MiG headed downward and burst into flame at about 35,000 feet. The pilot went down with his plane in the vicinity of the Chong Chone River. This action brought Hagerstrom's confirmed score to seven and one half enemy aircraft destroyed.

About the second week of May, Major Hagerstrom received orders to return to the United States. His scheduled departure on a MATS flight was delayed when SAC imposed its priority on the use of MATS aircraft, the duration of which was not announced. The personnel thus effected were instructed to be readily available at the airfield and prepared to depart at a moment's notice. On the second day of waiting, Major Hagerstrom, dressed in his blue uniform, was in the tactical flight operations office when the phone rang and his friend Bill Craig at the Joint Operations Center asked him if he could put up four planes right away. Jim replied that he would have them airborne in ten minutes. He quickly rounded up three pilots, made aircraft assignments and, without changing into a flight suit, strapped on a parachute and headed for the flight line. Jim took command of the flight, and off they went on a direct route to the north.

When about 30 miles south of the Yalu at 40,000 feet, they received instructions to turn to a heading of 270 degrees and were advised that a flight of MiGs was ahead of them. Hagerstrom ordered the auxiliary fuel tanks dropped and was informed of the miles remaining to intercept by the steady drone of the radar operator—36, 18, 12, 8 and lastly, 6 miles. Jim spotted the targeted formation of 24 MiGs flying about 4,000 feet above the Sabres, called control to report that he was having communications problems to prevent the possibility of a "recall" due to the high ratio of enemy aircraft to his own flight of four. While he was making his "report" he was also leading his flight in a climbing turn to the north to get above and behind the MiGs. His next turn placed the Sabres in a good attack position to the rear of the MiGs which were flying on a southeast heading. At this moment he saw the lead MiG enter a turn to the left which would soon place the enemy formation north of the Yalu and safety. The attack was initiated and Jim quickly took a MiG under fire, causing it to start smoking. His target entered a dive and Jim followed, firing short and accurate bursts as they descended. The leader of the enemy formation observed Hagerstrom's attack and dove in an attempt to get into firing position behind Jim, who quickly reversed course after being assured that he had destroyed his target and sped out of range of the attacking MiG leader. The Major then recalled his flight and headed for home. He also called control to report the number of enemy aircraft involved and requested that they scramble a large number of fighters as there were "enough MiGs up here for everyone."

Hagerstrom's downing of one MiG on this mission was confirmed by his wingman during the debriefing. While Jim was describing his aerial combat actions against the MiG he was interrupted by some shuffling sounds in the rear of the room and noticed that the pilot sitting next to him had moved in order to make room for Jim's commanding officer who sat down and said, "Jim, call operations and hold that C-54 because you are going to be on the first transport going home—and this is the one!"

Jim's homecoming reunion and leave with his wife and three children was enjoyed in Tyler, Texas, where the family remained after he departed for his new assignment in the Operations Section of the 9th Air Force at Pope Air Force Base, North Carolina. During September of 1953 Major Hagerstrom was selected to participate in the Bendix Air Race. He flew an F-86F from the 366th Tactical Fighter Wing which was stationed at England AFB, Louisiana. The race originated at Edwards AFB, California, with scheduled fuel stops at Colorado Springs, Colorado, and Olathe, Kansas. He crossed the finish line at Dayton, Ohio, just 30 seconds behind the winner.

Left: Major James P. Hagerstrom at the Bendix Air Race, 5 September 1953. (He placed 5th, just 30 seconds behind the winner.) Right: Lieutenant Colonel James P. Hagerstrom at Foster Air Force Base, 1955. (He flew the F-100 during this Tour of Duty.) Source of both: Hagerstrom Collection

Jim's well deserved promotion to Lieutenant Colonel came in June of 1954 followed by assignment as Commanding Officer of a Day Fighter Squadron which was stationed at Foster AFB in Texas. Six months later he was designated Inspector General for the Base— as an additional duty. A few months later the Wing Commander, Colonel Frank L. Dunn, designated Hagerstrom Group Commander and, concurrently, the Base Commander. Dunn's accompanying words were, "Let's see you straighten this Group up!"

Meeting that challenge, Lt. Colonel Hagerstrom quickly and efficiently rendered the Group "combat ready," won the Tactical Command Gunnery Competition, and represented Tactical Command at the Air Force Gunnery Competition at Nellis AFB. Upon his return to Foster from Nellis, Colonel Dunn rewarded Hagerstrom with command of the F-100 equipped 450th Day Fighter Group. From this assignment, Lt. Col. Hagerstrom was transferred to the Far East Air Force Headquarters (FEAF) at Fuji, Japan, as Chief of the Fighter Branch, where he remained until the latter part of 1956.

His next assignment was as an advisor to the Air National Guard (ANG) in Houston, Texas, where it is certain that his combat and command experience was of great value and benefit to those within the command which he was there to assist. While walking down the hall from his office enroute to another part of the headquarters one day, he was stopped by a general who exclaimed, "I don't believe this!" Hagerstrom replied, "You don't believe what, sir?" The general replied, "You're not dead and they just named an Air Base after you." It seemed that the ANG facility at Ellington, Texas, had been named, "Hagerstrom Field" and Jim had heard nothing about it.

Duty with the ANG did not last long. He was moved to Honolulu to join the staff of FEAF Headquarters which had been recently relocated to Hawaii from Japan. In March of 1959 James P. Hagerstrom was promoted to the rank of Colonel. While in Hawaii Jim earned a Master's Degree in Economics and departed Hawaii in 1960 for assignment as the Chief of Flight Safety of the Fighter Branch in the Norton AFB Headquarters. In addition to the normal work load of his office, he also pursued studies at the Loyola Law School in Los Angeles until he was selected for attendance at The Industrial College of the Armed Forces which required his transfer to the campus in Washington, DC. After getting settled in his new surroundings and regimen, Jim enrolled in the Georgetown University Law School. The thought of taking on two academic challenges at the same time is daunting, to say the east, but in 1964 he successfully graduated from the Industrial College on a Saturday and received his Law Degree from Georgetown during ceremonies on Sunday.

During 1965 Colonel Hagerstrom was assigned to the 7th Air Force in Saigon, Republic of Vietnam (RVN). He flew 30 combat missions during his tour of duty there and then was then transferred to Thailand where he remained until ordered to return to Norton AFB during the latter part of 1966. Shortly after his arrival at Norton, Jim took and passed the California Bar Examination, a truly amazing feat when one considers the demands of military duty and the dearth of time available for personal interests and pursuits during the rigorous duty assignments which he had experienced.

Colonel James P. Hagerstrom retired from the Air Force in January of 1968 after an exciting and dedicated career which spanned 27 years of distinguished and heroic service to his country which included active participation in three conflicts.

Life after departing the service was a series of unusual, interesting, and adventurous activities for the Hagerstrom family. Instead of moving to an area and home of their dreams, and perhaps starting a settled second career, as most are wont to do, Jim, his wife Lee and children, numbering five girls and three boys, spent the remainder of 1968 and half of 1969 living on a boat, traveling leisurely along the Pacific coast of Mexico. Upon return to the United States Jim began practicing law in San Diego and seemed quite content; however, thoughts of more travel are evidenced by the fact that the family started building their own boat in 1971—a 57 foot, 30 ton sailboat, which was completed and launched in 1975.

Jim took a leave of absence from his law firm at the end of 1975 and on 19 March 1976, the family sailed the boat to the west coast of Mexico. In May of that year an idyllic voyage to points of interest in the Pacific was started, with Hawaii as the initial destination. In the fall of 1976 they departed Hawaii and sailed through the Johnston Islands enroute to the Marshall Islands. While in the Marshalls, Jim was sworn into the bar of the "Trust Territory of the Pacific," the details and duties of which are not clear. Travel continued in early 1977, and shortly after arrival in the Carolina Islands, Jim became the District Attorney for the island called Kosrae, which is one of the eastern Carolinas.

The Hagerstroms then sailed to the island of Penapae, also in the Carolinas, in mid-1977. Jim opened a law practice and was recognized as the only attorney in the Carolina Islands during his stay. Their return to the United States during the summer of 1979 was somewhat temporary, as they decided to finally settle down in a Dominican Republic retirement setting and moved to Santo Domingo in 1980. They were very happy and content in their new home and surroundings until Jim succumbed to cancer on 25 June, 1993.

It is rare, indeed, that an individual can manage to do all of the things he wants to do over the course of his life and career and accomplish each with excellence. Colonel Hagerstrom seems to have realized all of his dreams and aspirations, which started with the desire to be a military aviator. He was a practicing attorney; he built and sailed his own boat and, importantly, spent several years on the boat with his family to make up for the long and frequent absences experienced while in the service. As a member of "The Inner Seven" he earned a special place in the annals of American aerial combat history as one of only seven aviators to become an "Ace" in piston driven and jet powered aircraft.

Colonel James P. Hagerstrom
United States Air Force, Retired
SN 0-727447 & 0-37787a

Awards And Decorations
Distinguished Service Cross
Silver Star
Legion of Merit
Distinguished Flying Cross with Two Oak Leaf Clusters
Air Medal with Ten Oak Leaf Clusters
USAF Commendation Medal

Service Medals
American Defense Service Medal
American Campaign Medal
Asiatic-Pacific Campaign Medal with Three Bronze Stars
World War II Victory Medal
National Defense Service Medal with One Bronze Star
Korean Service Medal with Two Bronze Stars
Longevity Service Award with Three Bronze Stars
Vietnam Service Medal
Armed Forces Reserve Medal

Citations
Distinguished Unit Citation with One Oak Leaf Cluster
Foreign Decorations
Republic of Korea Presidential Unit Citation
Vietnam Air Force Distinguished Flying Cross
Vietnam Air Force Medal of Honor

Foreign Decorations
United Nations Service Medal
Republic of Vietnam Campaign Medal

Credits For Enemy Aircraft Destroyed During Combat Actions

	Date	Aircraft Destroyed	Location
		World War II	
1943	11 April	1 Zeke	Oro Bay
	5 October	1 Dinah Madang	New Guinea
1944	23 January	4 1 Tony, 3 Hamp	Wewak, New Guinea
		Korea	
1952	21 November	1 MiG 15	Youngsi
	25 December	1 MiG 15	Sinsi-dong
1953	25 February	1 MiG 15	Konha-dong
	13 March	1.5 MiG 15	Wonson-Dong/Haksong-San
	27 March	2 MiG 15	Sanggyong-dong/Paeksang-ni
	13 April	1 MiG 15	Taegwan-dong
	16 May	1 MiG 15	Uiju

SUMMARY: Colonel Hagerstrom served in three conflicts and was one of the few of us who seemed to have achieved and enjoyed all of his life goals and objectives.

Official Record: 14.5 Enemy Aircraft Destroyed, 1 Probably Destroyed and 5 Damaged.

Across: Colonel James P. Hagerstrom at Norton Air Force, 1966. (Photo taken after completion of a four month Tour of Duty with the 7th Air Force in Saigon, Republic of Vietnam.) Source: Hagerstrom Collection

Photo of a painting of Major Harrison R. Thyng, West Hampnett, England,
Circa September 1942. Source: Thyng Collection

Chapter 6

Brigadier General Harrison R. Thyng

The history of this rare aviator and leader begins in the beautiful setting of rural New Hampshire in 1918. Harrison Reed Thyng was born on the 12th of April of that year in the town of Laconia, the second of Herbert and Elizabeth Thyng's two sons, and reared in nearby Barnstead. The nickname "Harry" was in use when he started school in the local one room school house, where instruction for all students from the 1st to 8th grade was provided by one teacher. While in the 8th grade, Harry performed the duties of school janitor in addition to keeping up with his studies.

He then attended the nearby Pittsfield High School where he played four years of football, one of them as team captain; he played four years of baseball and also was on the track team, lettering in all three sports. Graduation was celebrated in 1935, followed by matriculation at the University of New Hampshire at Durham, from which he received the Bachelor of Arts in Pre-Law Degree on 2 May 1939. He had also successfully completed four years of the Army ROTC Program and was commissioned a Second Lieutenant in the Infantry Branch of the United States Army Reserve upon graduation. Harry had worked his way through college, often spending up to 52 hours a week on part time jobs while at the same time meeting ROTC and college study and performance requirements.

Immediately after graduation Harry applied for the Army Air Corps Flying Cadet Program, was accepted, and sent to Parks Air College where Primary Flight Training was accomplished in the PT-13 aircraft. During Basic Training at Randolph Field, Texas, he flew the PT-13 and then moved into Advanced Training at Kelly Field, Texas. His class had a rare taste of "the old days" by being housed in WW I barracks but did have the benefit of flying the AT-6 as their qualification aircraft.

Harry Thyng graduated from flight training and received his "Wings" during ceremonies which were completed at 1100 hours on 23 March 1940. One hour later, in the Kelly Field Chapel, he married his long time sweetheart, Mary Rogers. There was no time for the traditional honeymoon as Harry departed the following day for six weeks of maneuvers with the 3rd Army in Georgia and South Carolina. On 1 May 1940, Lt. Thyng was assigned to the 94th Pursuit Squadron (PS) of the 1st Pursuit Group (PG) based at Selfridge Field, Michigan. He and his bride made themselves at home there as Harry sharpened his flying skills, and they both enjoyed the Michigan environment and duty station. On the 10th of October Harry was transferred to the 41st PS in the 31st PG. He was promoted to the rank of 1st Lieutenant on 1 November 1941.

Shortly after the United States entered WW II, the 41st FS was detached from the Group and 1st Lt. Harry Thyng was designated Commanding Officer of the 309th FS when it joined the 31st FG. The aircraft flown by the Group at that time was the P-39. Orders were soon received for the Group to relocate to England by flying their aircraft via the northern route to get there. This long flight was initiated in an orderly fashion, and all went well until the Group arrived at Grenier Field, New Hampshire. At some level of command, it was realized that the winter season had already arrived along the intended flight route, and the mission was delayed until plans for an alternative deployment were finalized.

The deployment solution was announced in April of 1942 when the 31st FG and its 307th, 308th and 309th Fighter Squadrons were ordered aboard a British cruiser with the destination of Glasgow, Scotland. After a relatively uneventful voyage, the group arrived in Scotland and was transported by train to England. The destination of the 309th was High

Ercall, Shropshire, with other Group elements based at nearby Atcham. The 31st was nicknamed "The Early Birds" of the 8th Air Force's newly formed 8th Fighter Command

With their assigned P-39s parked at Grenier Field, the pilots needed something to fly in order to be effective in stemming the German combat tide. With considerable skepticism, the 31st FG was quickly provided a full complement of British "Spitfire" fighters which had earned a sterling reputation in the ongoing Battle of Britain. The American pilots' concerns quickly turned to elation when they flew and realized the qualities and capabilities of the Spitfire. It had a speed of 408 miles per hour and a 660 mile radius of action, as well as excellent control response and maneuverability——features which exceeded the capabilities of American aircraft at that time.

After three weeks of training in the Spitfire, 1st Lt. Thyng led the first American fighter raids out of England. Harrison Thyng was promoted to Captain on 4 April 1942, and shortly thereafter he was ordered to relocate his squadron to West Hampnett, Sussex. This airfield was an RAF satellite installation within the Tangmere area, located about two miles from the English channel near the town of Chitchester. The 309th FS was quartered in two large houses near the airfield and provided rations in the form of a typically British diet of the times. Breakfast consisted of toast, tomatoes, and tea; dinner was usually Brussels sprouts. When meat was available, the slices were so thin that one could see right through them. Harry Thyng was promoted to the rank of Major on 15 June and remained in command of his squadron.

The 309th was the first squadron to be called upon when enemy aircraft came near the Tangmere area, and standing by on "alert" status became routine. Major Thyng's combat indoctrination came soon after getting settled at the new airfield when his squadron was "scrambled" to intercept approaching enemy aircraft. After takeoff he was told that the intruder was a Ju 88 and that he and his formation would be given a radar vector to intercept the target. We should note that radar was in a rudimentary stage of development at this time, as was the ability of pilots to fly in bad weather by use of cockpit flight instruments and navigational aids. The Spitfire pilots were thus limited to visual flight and avoided prolonged flight in clouds as often as possible.

The radar operator's directions placed Major Thyng in a position to spot and identify the intruding Ju 88. As he led his flight toward the enemy plane, he was startled by the number of what seemed to be fire flies that suddenly seemed to be all around the outside of his aircraft but soon realized that they were bullets being fired from the German plane. He then maneuvered into position behind the Ju 88, and while doing so, his wingman flew into a cloud formation and became separated from him. When within range, Harry fired a long burst which must have killed the tail gunner as he was not fired upon while at the closer range. Harry had also set the right engine of the Ju 88 ablaze and followed the burning plane through a cloud layer, placing more fire on it after they both broke out of the clouds.

At this point Harry was low on fuel and turned away to head for his home airstrip. Unfortunately, a filmed record of the engagement was not made. It seems that in the haste of the "scramble" Harry's crew chief had overlooked removal of the gun camera cover, and all that he could claim was a "probable." Despite the fact that personnel in the English radar station had monitored the German pilot's command for the crew to bail out and also saw his "blip" disappear from the screen, Major Thyng was not given official credit for this certain downing.

On 26 July Major Thyng participated in an RAF fighter sweep over the St. Omer and Abbeville areas. Official RAF missions for the 31st FG and its squadrons began on 5 August, followed some three weeks later with the initiation of command, control, and mission assignment by the 8th Air Force Fighter Command.

While returning from an escort mission on 19 August, as the 309th was over the English channel, one of the squadron pilots was forced to bail out of his Spitfire. Major Thyng ordered the remainder of his squadron to continue their homeward flight to West Hampnett while he remained with and provided protection for the pilot in the water until he was safely aboard a rescue boat. His low, circling, covering flight was undertaken despite the constant threat from marauding Me 109s. This was also the day that the English and Canadian Armies conducted the famous raid on Dieppe, with Major Thyng's squadron called upon to fly a total of four missions in support of that effort.

As the 8th Air Force continued to increase its bombing capability, the 31st FG was kept busy flying escort missions for the B-17s and A-20s which were based in England. The Battle of Britain had taken a heavy toll of RAF resources; thus English pilots rarely participated in these missions, apparently assigned to be the protective force for the home island. During these early months of air offense against targets on the European continent, the foe to friendly aircraft ratio was about 10 to 1, and survival depended upon the skill and daring of each Allied pilot and air crew committed to the mission effort, whether bomber, escort, or fighter sweep.

Under secret orders the 31st Fighter Group was designated one of the forces to participate in the invasion of North Africa which was code-named "Operation Torch," assigned to the XIIth Fighter Command, and transferred to Gibraltar with the mission of opening the air offensive in support of the North Africa invasion. On 23 October the Group personnel and equipment, less aircraft, departed England on a ship which was part of a large convoy. After a fourteen day voyage, normally accomplished in three, the 31st FG debarked at the port of Gibraltar on 6 November. Upon arrival at their assigned airfield, and to everyone's surprise, there was a full compliment of new desert camouflaged Spitfires already lined up on the parking ramp awaiting the Group's pilots and support personnel. The 31st immediately started flying missions over North Africa which consisted of strafing attacks on French tank and truck columns, artillery positions, and anti-aircraft gun emplacements. The frequent and persistent attacks by the Spitfires resulted in the destruction of many of the ground targets and disruption of the enemy's operations.

"Operation Torch" consisted of three main Allied assault landings in the areas of Oran (230 miles east of Gibraltar), Casablanca, and Algiers. The plan called for the 31st FG to fly from Gibraltar to the Oran sector, occupy the two airfields located there, refuel, and rapidly provide aerial support to ground operations. The airfields were named La Sena and Tafaroui, both of which were under Vichy French control. Tafaroui was considered the best of the two due to its paved runways.

Assault landings in the Oran and other sectors began at 0130 hours on 8 November. By the middle of the day the Casablanca and Algiers objectives were under Allied control, but the time schedule for taking the Oran area had been disrupted due to unanticipated enemy resistance. In mid-afternoon the belly tank equipped 31st FG was dispatched to Oran. According to the plan, it was calculated that both of the airfields there would be secured by the time the 31st arrived, and the way cleared for the relocation of additional groups and squadrons to support the offensive to the east.

The 31st FG, with Major Thyng's 309th FS in the lead, took off from Gibraltar at 1540 hours and reached Oran a little before sunset. Upon arrival over Oran, the squadron found four Vichy piloted Dewoitine 520 fighter planes milling around the area and reported the situation. The 31st FG was instructed not to fire on the French aircraft, which resembled an American P-51B, had a maximum speed of 408 mph, a 43,000 foot operating ceiling, and were certainly no match for the Spitfire. Thyng was suspicious of the intent and purpose of the enemy planes and advised the Group Commander that he would keep the flight he was leading airborne to fly cover while the remainder of the Group and his squadron landed. This was a prudent decision as the Vichy fighters attacked the last formation while on its landing approach and shot down the trail aircraft. Major Thyng immediately interceded with his flight of four, which shot down three of the four Vichy planes during a violent set of dog fights. Thyng had taken the Vichy flight leader as his target and dispatched the plane and pilot in flames at about five hundred feet of altitude near the airfield. This was Harry's first credited enemy aircraft downing.

Major Thyng's flight joined the rest of his squadron on Tafaroui, landing out of ammunition, nearly out of fuel and, along with the other members of the 31st, found that the American ground forces had not yet secured the Oran airfields. This meant that there was no security, no fuel, no food, and no ground personnel. It is indeed fortunate that the enemy had evacuated this area in advance of the approaching Allied Forces and the arrival of the 31st! There was, however, a total of 90 Dewoitine 520's parked on the occupied airfields, and after a considerable draining, carrying and pouring effort during the night, they provided sufficient fuel to ready four Spitfires for missions at first light. During the early morning darkness the American fliers were rudely awakened by the noise of explosions and anti-aircraft fire, the source and purpose of which could not be determined. This did little to ease the minds and answer the many questions of the aviators who were isolated from friendly forces.

Harry Thyng took off on patrol at the break of dawn on 9 November and, after an uneventful flight, returned to Tafaroui to find that the Allied Forces had still not arrived. On his second patrol of the day, Harry discovered and reported a German armored force advancing toward Allied positions from the direction of Sidi-Bel-Abbes. He personally destroyed several tracked vehicles and trucks in the face of heavy enemy protective ground fire before returning safely to Tafaroui. It was soon learned that the column which he attacked was actually the famed French Foreign Legion. The damage inflicted was sufficient to cause the Legion to turn south, which eliminated their immediate threat to the Allied ground forces.

American Army elements finally arrived in the Oran area during the early afternoon of 10 November with the supplies, ground crew, and support personnel so vitally needed by the 31st FG and its squadrons. In mid-afternoon General Doolittle arrived, unexpectedly, to make a first-hand assessment of the situation at the two forward operating airfields as related to Air Force capabilities to support ground operations and simultaneously thwart Luftwaffe interference.

November 11th was marked by the signing of an Allied armistice with the Vichy French. This effectively denied the German forces any further organized assistance from their recent host and ally. However, the tempo of air operations rapidly increased as more Allied air power joined the 31st and the Luftwaffe countered with notable aggressiveness.

Desert weather conditions soon became a matter of concern, consideration, and challenge to the combatants. Dust storms which contained high winds and caused severely reduced visibility would last for hours and sometimes days. While the ground forces would for the most part "button up" for the duration of the storms, the air forces of both sides continued their offensive operations through, above, and around the huge clouds of blowing sand. It became a deadly game to see which side's aircraft could return to its base to refuel, rearm, have the aircraft cleaned and return to the air in hopes of catching the adversary's aircraft on the ground. Neither side was successful in this quest up to the point which led Major Thyng to order a shortcut to his squadron, "Just refuel, rearm, get back in the air, and catch them on the ground this time!"

The results of this tactic were not recorded, but of the eleven attacking 309th Spitfires, the one flown by Harry Thyng was the only one which did not return to Tafaroui that day. The Major had crash-landed behind enemy lines. Other than a bad gash on his head, which bled profusely, he was able to orient himself and plan his next move. As soon as darkness fell, Harry started walking through the desert toward friendly lines in an effort to rejoin his squadron. He identified the enemy side of the lines by a tent and a small structure which were spaced about four hundred yards apart. No activity could be heard or observed; Harry proceeded very cautiously until he could see a relaxing sentry at each location, at which time he started crawling on his hands and knees from a point between the two sentry posts, which turned out to be manned by half-hearted Italian troops. Movement was slow, and it was daylight by the time he was about two hundred yards past the sentry line and somewhat out of sight due to the gently rolling dunes.

The young major was startled by an Arab who appeared out of nowhere, pointed at him and shouted, "Shoot him!" Harry immediately started running as fast as he could, accompanied by the cracking noise of bullets all around him. Fortunately he wasn't hit, and after an exhausting mile or so was surprised when he crested a sand dune and discovered a camel train accompanied by about twelve dogs headed in the direction from which he had just come. As soon as he was spotted, one of the Arabs got off his camel and, accompanied by the dogs, started walking in Harry's direction.

American pilots had been warned that the Arabs had been promised a large reward for the safe delivery of Allied pilots by the Americans and the Germans, with no differentiation made as to which side they should be delivered. In Thyng's case it obviously would have been to the Germans. The other admonition to aviators was that they should never shoot or shoot at Arab dogs. The appropriateness of these two pieces of information certainly applied to Harry's present situation but in no way could provide a solution to the immediate problems he faced.

Harry was armed with the standard Army .45 caliber pistol, and he noted that the Arabs carried very old rifles. The dogs broke into a run and attacked the unfortunate airman, who immediately fired several shots at the dogs and started running as fast as he could in the direction of friendly forces. The dogs did not pursue Harry nor did the Arabs, for some reason, follow or shoot at him as he fled. He was soon over the crest of a dune and out of sight of his potential captors. After resuming a walking pace, Harry heard the sound of an approaching vehicle and was greatly relieved when an American tank came into view and effected his rescue. The armored unit to which the tank was assigned provided him with transportation to his home airfield, where he rejoined his squadron. That evening he was pleasantly amused to hear the radio broadcast which announced the capture of Major Harrison E. Thyng by the enemy. Harry Thyng was back in the air the next morning.

Units of the U.S. 8th Army advanced into Tunisia on 4 February 1943. The rapid advance of ground forces dictated that the 31st FG relocate forward to the airfield at Thelepte near the western border of Tunisia. The move was accomplished on 6 February. During the morning of 15 February, while leading his squadron on a mission to Pichon, Major Thyng monitored a radio call that German fighters were strafing the strip from which he had just departed. He immediately changed course to return to his home base and drive off the attackers. As he approached Thelepte, Harry targeted one of the strafing Messerschmitts and quickly sent it down in flames. The remainder of the German formation scattered and departed the area.

On 17 February General Erwin Rommel, "The Desert Fox," launched a surprise attack against the Allies spearheaded by the 15th Panzer Division, quickly taking Gafsa, which is close to the Algerian/Tunisian border junction and about fifty miles from the infamous

Kasserine Pass. The depth of this attack to the west caused five of the XIIth Air Force's forward airfields to be abandoned upon very short notice. The 31st FG moved from Thelepte to a makeshift airstrip at Tebessa and due to insufficient warning of the move, some valuable equipment had to be left behind. On 21 February Rommel's forces breached the Kasserine Pass and threatened to fan out into the valley occupied by the Allies. This caused the 31st to leave Tebessa and occupy the airstrips located at Youks-les-Bains and Le Kouie, which were northwest of Thelepte on the eastern border of Algeria.

During the month of March, the 31st FG was employed in the conduct of fighter sweeps and escort missions for A-20s, B-25s, and B-26s. During the second mission of 4 March, Major Thyng was leading two squadrons of Spitfires over LaFauconnerie, Tunisia, as high cover for a formation of light bombers. Shortly after his covering force had been attacked by Me 109s, he noticed that one of the bombers had been badly damaged by anti-aircraft fire and led his flight of four fighters out of the formation to provide protective escort to the disabled ship enroute to its home base. It was necessary for his small force to fight off the Messerschmitts which were attempting to finish off the disabled bomber during the homeward journey, which was accomplished successfully with no further damage being done to the bomber and none to the escorting aircraft.

The Group occupied the airfield at Cap Bon during late March and was given the new and interesting additional mission of flying to an island by the name of Pantelleria, which lay halfway between Cap Bon and Sicily, in an effort to entice the German and Italian pilots into the air for a fight, a technique which was often successful. On 29 March while leading a flight on a fighter sweep to Pantelleria, Major Thyng shot down the first of the enemy aircraft to be encountered, a FW 190. On 1 April, while leading a flight of 12 Spitfires to the island, he was engaged by a large force of fighters. During the ensuing brace of individual encounters, Thyng chased one Me 109 opponent into the water. As he pulled out of his dive, Harry saw four descending parachutes, a mute testimony as to how well the pilots of his squadron had performed. He led his flight home with no damage or losses suffered by the Americans.

Harrison E. Thyng was promoted to the rank of Lieutenant Colonel on 18 April 1943, just six days after his 25th birthday, and placed in command of the 31st Fighter Group. One must reflect upon the career of this young officer up to this time. Commissioned on 24 March 1940, he was promoted to First Lieutenant on 1 November 1941 and placed in command of a fighter squadron—a position normally held by a major or lieutenant colonel. As recognition of his extraordinary leadership skills and capabilities, he received highly accelerated promotions after assuming command of the 309th: First Lieutenant to Captain—8 months, Captain to Major—just under 3 months, Major to Lieutenant Colonel—10 months, all while commanding the same organization! It is not certain if this achievement is a record, but it must be very close to one.

Details of the mission of 6 May were not recorded, but Thyng was credited with the destruction of one Me 109 on that date. His personal narrative indicated that he was shot down by British flak while shooting down that Me 109. He parachute-landed between the lines and was picked up by the occupants of a British jeep type vehicle. He had suffered fragment wounds from the flak and a broken back (the cause of which was not disclosed, and leads to speculation as to whether it was during the aircraft exit or during the parachute landing). Enroute to his unit the British jeep was driven over a steep embankment and Harry was thrown out of the vehicle, adding a broken ankle to his list of wounds. Lt. Col. Harry Thyng was medically treated and then returned to the USA in early June. He was a recognized "Ace" with credit for the destruction of five enemy aircraft, two "probables" and three "damaged" during the 162 combat missions he had flown.

After a long rest he was assigned as the commander of an air base near Naples, Florida. Not content with this type of duty while a war was in progress, he volunteered for overseas duty during 1944. His application was accepted and Harry was immediately directed to organize, activate, train and command a long range fighter group which would be equipped with the P-47N aircraft. This fighter had the most welcome capability of flying fourteen hours without refueling. The new organization, the 413th Long Range Fighter Group (LRFG), was formed and trained at Bluthenthall, North Carolina; when declared combat ready the group was processed for overseas movement, less aircraft, with scheduled transportation to Hawaii. Twenty-six year old Group Commander Harry Thyng was promoted to the rank of Colonel on 24 February 1945.

Upon arrival in Hawaii, the Group was equipped with 75 new P-47Ns and dispatched on the first single engine fighter plane crossing of the Pacific, "island hopping" from Hawaii to the small island of Ie Shima, which is located west of Okinawa and boasted a 6,000 foot coral surfaced runway. It was here that celebrated war correspondent Ernie Pyle was killed earlier in the war.

The 413th FG flew long range escort missions for the B-29 bomber formations which were normally of 8-10 hours in duration, generally to Kyushu, Japan, and as far as Tokyo. While on a strafing run south of Kyushu Harry and the others in his formation saw the huge mushroom cloud caused by the detonation of the second atomic bomb which was dropped on Japan and hastened the end of World War II. This observation and credit for probably downing an Oscar were the highlights of the 22 combat missions he flew while commanding the 413th.

From the Pacific Theater Colonel Thyng was returned to the United States and, after taking leave, assigned to 5th Air Force Headquarters in San Antonio, Texas. He joined the Regular Army on 5 July 1946, and on 30 June 1947 his Colonelcy was terminated. In response to his request, Harry was designated Senior Instructor for the 101st Wing of the Air National Guard (ANG) which encompassed the states of Maine, New Hampshire and Vermont, and reported to his new assignment on 27 September 1947. Each of these states added an ANG element to their traditional Army structure and activated one P-47 equipped fighter squadron per state. He was re-appointed to the rank of Colonel on 12 September 1948. While with the ANG, Colonel Thyng stayed deeply involved with the evolution of combat capabilities in the Air National Guard and enjoyed the three years he spent overseeing the progress of the units in his charge. One of the high points of this tour was the assignment of F-80 fighters to the squadron which was based at Dow Field in Bangor, Maine. He lost no time in obtaining a local check-out in this new and exciting aircraft and had accumulated 300 hours by the time his tour came to a close. He was affectionately designated "Father of the New England ANG Wing" upon his departure.

On 30 March 1951 Harry assumed Command of the 33rd Fighter Wing at Otis Air Force Base, Massachusetts, where he enjoyed the duty and the Cape Cod surroundings. This tour of duty was short lived, however, as he received orders to Korea and departed Otis on 15 September. His orders designated him Commander of the 4th Fighter Interceptor Wing (FIW) which was already in Korea. The distinguished history of the 4th FIW dates back to the fall of 1942 when it was activated as the 4th FG under 8th Air Force in England and was composed of the 71st, 121st and 133rd Fighter Squadrons. The 4th is mentioned in other chapters of this book.

At the time of Colonel Thyng's assumption of command on 6 November 1951, the 4th FIW was the only F-86 "Saber Jet" equipped command in Korea. It should be noted, however, that Harry had arrived in Korea well ahead of this date and had flown missions prior to joining the Wing. On 24 October Col. Thyng led a flight of F-86s into North Korea. In the vicinity of Sinanju at approximately 1510 hours, he observed a flight of nine MiGs on a southerly heading with the obvious intention of attacking a formation of friendly fighter bombers. At an altitude at which the MiG 15 had superior climbing ability, Thyng led his flight in the attack against a formation which now numbered 11 MiGs, as two more had joined the original 9. Harry took the first MiG under fire, causing parts to fly off the aircraft, the pilot to eject, and the pilotless plane to crash.

With the formalities of command assumption——getting to know his staff and subordinate commanders, and establishing priorities and procedures——quickly accomplished, Colonel Thyng was in the air with his command as often as possible. On 23 November while leading a squadron of Sabre Jets over North Korea, Harry spotted a formation of 10 MiG 15s flying toward friendly fighter bombers which were attacking rail supply lines. He initiated an aggressive attack and was startled when, a few seconds later, his wingman reported his aircraft had been badly damaged and that he was still under attack. Harry quickly maneuvered into a position to fire on the attacking MiG. Harry's accurate burst at very close range was followed by his pressing of the diving attack to such a low altitude that the MiG could not recover, and crashed. Unfortunately, his wingman had, by this time, also crashed. Although low on fuel and in an area infested with MiGs, Harry remained in the area as long as possible looking for the spot where his wingman went down and any sign of life.

Harry related the story of the foregoing mission to the author during an interview conducted in 1982. He stated, "Fighter pilots have a tendency to fly hard, fight hard, and play hard. This was particularly true in Korea; there was generally an uproar in the Officers Club, especially in the early evening. With the many prominent visitors we had, I felt the club should be calmed down a bit. Harry Thyng threw himself out of the club for thirty days, and surprisingly enough the club was in fine shape after that."

At 0850 on 14 December while leading a flight of four Sabres, Colonel Thyng spotted a formation of four MiG 15s in the vicinity of Yonh' Ang-Dong which were flying at a lower altitude and seemingly unaware of his presence. He led his flight in an attacking dive and selected the plane in the number three position as his target. His long burst of fire raked the fuselage and caused the enemy aircraft to burst into flame and crash.

On 10 March 1952 Harry was again leading a flight of four Sabres on a fighter bomber escort mission near the mouth of the Yalu River with his flight divided into two elements for greater flexibility and coverage. At approximately 1220 he came upon six MiG 15s which were attacking an RF-80 and its four F-86 escorts. He immediately dove to the attack, and at 10,000 feet took one of the attackers under fire, observing good hits in the engine area and resultant trail of smoke from the exhaust. He quickly maneuvered into another firing position. His second burst caused the MiG to explode and the wreckage fall to earth. The remainder of the disorganized MiG 15s fled to safety north of the Yalu. Successful completion of the RF-80 reconnaissance mission was attributed to Harry's timely and aggressive intervention in what could have been a serious defeat of the small force which was under enemy attack.

April 18th was another victorious day for Harry Thyng. While leading a flight of four Sabres near the major Antung Airfield, Harry spotted two MiG 15s taking off to the south and entered a diving turn to position his flight behind them. At high speed and close range Colonel Thyng fired a long burst at the number two aircraft. The hits in the fuselage area resulted in the canopy being jettisoned, but before the pilot could eject the MiG went out of control and crashed near Yansi. This was Harry's fourth confirmed MiG 15 downing.

Colonel Harry R. Thyng (right), Commander of the 4th Fighter Interceptor Wing at Kimpo (K-14) Air Base, Korea, 1952, with unidentified Airman.
Source: USAF File Photo

Harry was the leader of a flight of two Sabres on 20 May in the vicinity of In' Gok-Tong. At 1340 he spotted two MiGs flying at a lower altitude and initiated the attack. While he and his wingman were firing on the two target MiGs, they were taken under fire by an element of MiGs which they had not seen. Harry executed an abrupt tight right turn into the attackers which caused them to break sharply upward and to the left. The violence of the maneuver caused one of the MiGs to climb in a tight spiral, emit smoke and vapor, and then enter a high speed dive from which it did not recover. It crashed and exploded near In' Gok Tong, with Colonel Thyng credited with the downing, his fifth in Korea, which made him the 16th "Jet Ace" of the Korean Conflict and the fourth member of "The Inner Seven."

Colonel Harry Thyng relinquished command of the 4th FIW on 2 October and departed for the United States on the same day. After taking the customary leave, he reported to Hamilton Field, just north of San Francisco, on 7 December 1952 and was assigned as the Deputy Commander for Operations of the Western Air Defense Command. On 12 June 1954 Harry became Commander of the 4702nd Air Defense Wing at Geiger Air Force Base, Spokane, Washington. During this tour of duty, Harry was inducted into the "Caterpillar Club" as the result of hail damage to the T-33 he was flying. The hail was so severe that he was forced to eject and safely ride his parachute back to earth. (It should be noted that membership in the "Caterpillar Club" is restricted to those pilots who have parachuted from the aircraft they were flying when continued flight was impossible or inadvisable.)

Colonel Thyng was appointed Division Commander of the 9th Air Division, also at Geiger, on 8 October 1954. On 10 January 1955 Harry was further elevated to the position of Vice Commander of the 9th Air Division and remained in this position until 1 July 1957 when he departed to become a student at the National War College in Washington, D.C. Upon graduation from the War College in July of 1958, Harry was assigned to Air Force Headquarters as Chief of the Allocations Division. On 5 January 1959 Harry was assigned to the Jet Plans Division of the Federal Aviation Agency and remained in Washington until 25 September 1960.

From October 1960 through May of 1963, Colonel Thyng served as Commander of the Duluth Air Defense Sector. Harrison E. Thyng was promoted to the rank of Brigadier General on 29 May 1963, which he described as, "My most memorable, happy day was the day I pinned 2nd Lt. gold bars on my son Jim as he graduated from the Air Force Academy, and he in turn pinned a star on each of my shoulders denoting my promotion to Brigadier General." General Thyng next became the Deputy Commander of the Northern Region, North American Air Defense Command (NORAD), and his final assignment was as Commander of the Washington Air Defense Sector (WADS) at Fort Lee Air Force Station, Virginia, retiring with honors on 31 March 1966.

Throughout his 27 years of dedicated and distinguished service, Harry was noted for his outstanding flying skills and leadership ability. Few officers have experienced the assumption of command as young as did Harry Thyng and consistently commanded most of the organizations to which he was assigned from First Lieutenant through the rank of Brigadier General. It is not known if he holds the record for the most time spent in command positions during a career, but it would seem that his record would be difficult to beat. One of the aviators who flew with Harry in combat attested to his leadership by simply stating, "I'll follow him anywhere!"

After retirement Harry and his wife Mary returned to New Hampshire and settled in Pittsfield, the setting of his youth. With a strong desire to continue serving his nation, Harry quickly started campaigning and was a nominated Republican candidate for election to the U.S. Senate. Although not elected during the vote which was taken in November of 1966, the narrow margin of his loss after only six months or so of campaigning in the totally unfamiliar field of politics and as a stranger in his home state spoke highly of his charisma and sincerity, which certainly impressed the voters.

His public spirit undaunted, Harry founded the New England Aeronautical Institute, which later became Daniel Webster Junior College. He successfully served as its president from 1967 through 1972 and was credited with major improvements in all areas of operation during his tenure. Harry's energy seems to have been boundless. He was an active member of the local Masonic Lodge, Order of Daedalians, and as a Charter Member of the American Fighter Aces Association also served as its Vice President and Secretary-Treasurer. His hobbies included hunting, fishing, water and snow skiing, golf, bowling, and

Retired Brigadier General Harry Thyng with his wife Mary and President Dwight D. Eisenhower during his narrowly lost campaign for United States Senate in New Hampshire, 1966. Source: Thyng Collection

curling. Interests were pursued in the areas of writing a book about his military experiences and cataloging photos and souvenirs collected during the many years of his service. He also enjoyed spending as much time as possible with his wife, children, and grandchildren as well as driving the 1931 Model "A" Ford which he fully restored.

Harry may have retired from the Air Force but certainly fit the description of being "gone but not forgotten," as indicated by the humorous story which he related during an interview conducted by the author in 1982: "One evening during the Panama Canal crisis in the fall of 1979, I had gone up to bed, and Mary was puttering around downstairs when the phone rang. When Mary answered, a voice said that it was the White House calling and asked for me. Well, we have several good friends who are practical jokers, and Mary figured that the caller was one of those just pulling our leg. She could have said that I was upstairs in bed reading a Playboy magazine but just told the caller that I was upstairs asleep and then hung up the phone. The incident slipped Mary's mind, and she didn't mention it at breakfast. At about nine o'clock the phone rang, and it was New Hampshire's Senator MacIntyre who immediately asked why I didn't answer the call from the White House last night and said that they would call again shortly. Mary then explained what had happened, and I waited for the call. Sure enough, the next call was from the White House, and at the end of the conversation, the man in Washington concluded by saying , "That's some stupid maid you have to hang up on the White House!"

(Harry did not reveal the purpose or results of the call, and this writer didn't ask .)

Harry and Mary Thyng enjoyed their lives in rural New Hampshire, making the most of each day, both together and while pursuing their individual interests. Harry died on 29 September 1983. In accordance with his request, the cause of his death was not disclosed. He was truly a great American patriot whose personal examples of dedication and skill, coupled with the highest quality leadership applications, certainly touched and positively influenced the lives of the thousands with whom he came in contact during his outstanding military and post-retirement careers.

Brigadier General Harrison R. Thyng
United States Air Force, Retired
SN 0-376197 & 0-33996

Awards And Decorations
Silver Star with Two Oak Leaf Clusters
Legion of Merit with Two Oak Leaf Clusters
Distinguished Flying Cross with Three Oak Leaf Clusters
Purple Heart
Air Medal with Thirty-three Oak Leaf Clusters
USAF Commendation Medal

Service Medals
American Defense Service Medal
American Campaign Medal
Asiatic-Pacific Campaign Medal with Four Battle Stars
European-African-Middle East Campaign Medal with Four Battle Stars
World War II Victory Medal
Army of Occupation Medal (Japan)
National Defense Service Medal
Air Force Longevity Service Award with One Silver Oak Leaf Cluster
Korean Service Medal with Three Bronze Stars

Citations
Presidential Unit Citation
Distinguished Unit Citation

Foreign Decorations
French Croix De Guerre
United Nations Service Medal

Credits For Enemy Aircraft Destroyed During Combat Actions

Date		Aircraft Destroyed	Location
		World War II	
1942	8 November	1 D 520	Tafaroui
1943	15 February	1 Me 109	Thelepte
	29 March	1 FW 190	El Guettar
	1 April	1 Me 109	U-2073 to Y-7684
	6 May	1 Me 109	K-1035 Area
		Korea	
1951	24 October	1 MiG 15	Sananju
	14 December	1 MiG 15	Yonh' Ang-Dong
1952	10 March	1 MiG 15	Mouth of Yalu River
	18 April	1 MiG 15	Over North Korea
	20 May	1 MiG 15	In' Gok-tong

SUMMARY: The only member of "The Inner Seven" to reach General Officer rank, Harry continued to make major contributions to the nation during his second career and retired life. **Official Record:** 10 Enemy Aircraft Destroyed, 3 Probably Destroyed and 7 Damaged.

Across: Newly promoted Captain Harry Thyng, Commanding Officer of the 309th Fighter Squadron, in the Cockpit of a British Spitfire at High Ercall, England, April 1942. Source: Thyng Collection

Major Bill Whisner upon return from the 26 September 1951 mission during which a 4th Fighter Interceptor Wing Contingent of 34 Sabre Jets flew against 70 MiGs. Source: USAF File Photo

Chapter 7

Colonel William T. Whisner, Junior

William T. Whisner, Jr. was the youngest of "The Inner Seven." The heroic and skillful aerial combat exploits and achievements which follow were recorded during World War II and the Korean Conflict and may seem rather amazing in light of his rather modest and reserved upbringing.

Bill Whisner was born in Shreveport, Louisiana, on 17 October 1923. During his youth he was active in the Boy Scouts and achieved the rank of Eagle Scout, the highest awarded in Scouting. While attending Byrd High School, he joined the Junior Reserve Officer Training Corps (JROTC), and it was during this time that he made the decision to become a military aviator.

Immediately upon graduation from high school, he applied for the Army Air Force Cadet Program, was accepted, and on 8 April 1942, at the age of 18, became a Cadet. His Primary Training was received in Lafayette, Louisiana, where he learned to fly in PT-17s and PT-19s. Upon successful completion of this phase, he underwent Basic Training at Greenville, Mississippi, and was then sent to Napier Field, Alabama, where he flew AT-6s during Advanced Training. Bill was commissioned a Second Lieutenant and received his pilot rating on 16 February 1943. His very proud mother, Mrs. Eloise Whisner, was present to "pin on" his bars and wings.

The teenaged Lieutenant was then sent to Westover Field, Massachusetts, for Operational Training in the Republic P-47 "Thunderbolt." From Westover he was assigned to the 34th Fighter Squadron (FS) at LaGuardia Field, New York. This unit was later redesignated the 487th Fighter Squadron (FS) of the 352nd Fighter Group (FG); both of which were nearing the completion of Stateside training prior to being shipped overseas.

The 352nd FG Headquarters and its assigned squadrons boarded the *Queen Elizabeth* enroute to England in June of 1943. Upon arrival the Group occupied the Bodney Airfield in East Anglia where the initial months were totally occupied with training flights over England and acclimatization to flying in the unfamiliar European weather. The 352nd FG was declared "combat ready" on 9 September 1943 and flew its first combat mission on that date.

The following four months produced no spectacular results for the 352nd FG. The Thunderbolts were limited in range, and there were not that many enemy aircraft within their range to provide a major confrontation with the Luftwaffe. However, the Group did achieve a modest combat record of 23 confirmed enemy aircraft destroyed, 2 aircraft probably destroyed, and 2 damaged.

By late January of 1944 the 8th Fighter Command, to which the 352nd FG was assigned, had developed a new plan for the protective escort of the bomber force which would provide continuous support for the bombers to and from their target destinations. Each of the shorter range P-47 Thunderbolt Groups was assigned a definite area along the bomber routes to provide escort to all of the bomb groups which passed through. Once the bombers' Initial Point (IP) (an identifiable point on the ground) was reached, the long range P-38s and P-51s took over and escorted the bombers throughout the bomb run and initial leg home. They were then relieved by the P-47s which had escort responsibility for the sector through which the returnees would fly.

The plan was first tried on the mission of 24 January, but bad weather disrupted the mission, and the results were inconclusive. Several encounters did take place, however, and 8th FC pilots downed 19 enemy fighters at the cost of nine of their own. The extended escort plan was executed again on 29 January 1944 with better and more conclusive results. On this mission, twelve P-47 Thunderbolt fighter groups from the 8th FC and one P-51 Mustang group from the 9th FC escorted three bomber divisions during the attack on Frankfurt. This time they found the fight they were looking for.

Air battles raged throughout the penetration, bombing, and withdrawal stages of the mission, and the result was a decisive victory for the American pilots with enemy aircraft losses set at 47 destroyed and 5 probables as compared to the American loss of 14 fighters. One of the groups which played a large part in this victory was the 352nd FG with a score of 6-0-1. This mission signaled a new beginning for the Group in general and for Lt. Bill Whisner of the 487th Fighter Squadron in particular. One of the air battles was already raging when the 352nd arrived at the rendezvous point over Belgium. The bombers were being harassed by a "gaggle" of enemy fighters as they passed over Namur, and the 352nd fighters rushed to their rescue. Up to this date Lt. Whisner, who flew as Captain George Preddy's wingman, had not had an opportunity to engage an enemy fighter; however, this time he would not be denied. The Thunderbolts charged into the enemy fighters and individual dogfights broke out all over the sky. Bill Whisner got his first chance about ten minutes after the initial contact when he observed two FW 190s hacking away at a B-17 Flying Fortress formation. He pushed his Thunderbolt into a shallow dive and chose his target but too late to save one of the Fortresses under attack, which fell out of formation. Bill was determined that at least one FW 190 pilot would not attack another B-17, and hit the 190 with a short burst of his fifties and then followed him down to about 1,000 feet. The enemy pilot began twisting and climbing in an attempt to evade his pursuer, but Lt. Whisner caught him with another burst, which was quickly followed by still another as his adversary was diving away through a layer of clouds. The enemy pilot jumped from his non-flyable aircraft at about 800 feet, and Lt. Whisner claimed the first of many air victories which would follow during his career.

While equipped with the P-47 Thunderbolt, the 352nd FG was not considered particularly successful in the eyes of senior Air Corps leaders. The destruction of 63 enemy aircraft during the initial seven months of combat flying was below the unspecified number the Group had been expected to achieve. Such factors as range, method of employment, and opportunity had obviously not been included in this expectation-driven anticipation.

The entire 352nd was re-equipped with the sleek, long-nosed, P-51 "Mustang" in late March of 1944. In the words of Bob Powell, who was there, "As was the custom, each aircraft underwent the ritual of having a pet name painted on the fuselage. In Whisner's case, however, he was forced to name his plane "Princess Elizabeth," an act concocted by our Public Relations Office and enforced by Colonel Joe Mason, the commander——an order and a name which Bill thoroughly detested. This was in anticipation of an invitational visit by the Princess, and the "Command desire" for her to see a P-51 named in her honor. The morning she was scheduled to make her visit the aircraft were lined up wingtip to wingtip (a great target for the Germans had they happened upon the scene). The ship next to Bill's "Princess" was Cy Doleac's plane with the humorous inscription, "EXLAX, Shh't and Git." When Joe Mason came out and saw that he nearly had a coronary. In his booming voice he yelled for his crew chief to get that blankety-blank plane off the line, NOW! A half-track pulled the plane away just minutes before "Princess" came onto the field."

At about the time the P-51s were received, 8th Air Force published a directive that each Group would have its own colors for both morale and identification purposes. As related by Bob Powell, "Our Group got the color blue for application to the nose of each aircraft. One of the artistic mechanics on the flight line came up with the design which swept blue back from the nose to the canopy and downward at the front of the nose. However, we really got the nickname Bluenosers started when someone paraphrased General Hermann Goering's remarks to the effect that he would know that Germany had lost the war when he saw Mustangs over Berlin. Someone in the outfit changed the wording slightly to say '—when he saw the Bluenosed Bastards of Bodney over Berlin.' That did it! The Group was thereafter known as the "Bluenosers."

The 352nd's fortunes immediately changed for the better with the P-51s. Within the first two weeks of April while flying the new Mustangs, the 352nd FG destroyed 28 enemy aircraft in aerial combat and numerous others on the ground. Lt. Bill Whisner was one of the pilots involved in the April victory spree. His first opportunity to add to his score came on 9 April when the Group was on an escort mission over Belgium while he was flying as wingman to Captain Preddy. Shortly after arriving at the rendezvous point the Group passed over a grass airfield which contained several twin engine German aircraft. Captain Preddy led his flight in a diving attack against this lucrative target. As the Mustangs hurtled earthward, a panel in Lt. Whissner's cockpit canopy burst. Thinking he had been hit by enemy fire Whisner pulled up. After realizing what had actually happened, he resumed his attack. He made a total of five passes over the field, and by the time he had finished, his tally was two Ju 88s destroyed along with a damaged barracks building which was located near the burning enemy bombers. The attack on the ground installation and parked aircraft resulted in 11 of the Ju 88s left burning, and unassessed building damage. This destruction, along with a successful aerial engagement by Lt. Long of the 328th FS, and a "probable" by Major Willie Jackson, gave the 352nd FG a total of 12-1-0 for the day.

Prior to the end of April, the Bluenosers continued their rampage and claimed a score of 107-4-62 for the month, seven of which were aircraft destroyed in the air with one of them credited to Lt. Bill Whisner during the engagement of 30 April. The next action came while the 352nd was escorting a formation of B-17s during a bombing mission on the airfield at Clermont-Ferrand, France. Whisner spotted an FW 190 trying to sneak in on one of the B-17s and reported the enemy aircraft over the radio as he peeled off to attack this target, some 2,000 feet below him. He over-anxiously opened fire at too great a range which resulted in a miss. The enemy pilot, thus alerted, dove for the deck hotly followed by Whisner, who was covered by the remainder of his section. During the high speed dive Whisner fired and missed a second time, just before his adversary pulled out of his dive and flew directly over the targeted airfield at about 100 feet of altitude. At this point, Lt. Whisner, flying Lt. Colonel John Meyer's *Lambie II*, began closing rapidly and opened fire at 100 yards. His bullets ripped large chunks of metal from the 190, which immediately lost airspeed and headed downward. The credit to Whisner for a destroyed aircraft was confirmed by Captain Clayton Davis who reported seeing a raging fire at the location where the enemy aircraft should have crashed.

During the month of May, the 352nd FG continued punishing the Germans wherever and whenever they could be found, both in the air and on the ground. On 8 May the Bluenosers recorded 27-2-7 enemy planes in aerial combat against one loss and claimed another 10-0-2 on 12 May. It was during the latter mission that Bill Whisner added to his score by destroying a Ju 87 during a strafing run on the Frankenhausen Airfield. Aerial encounters had eluded Bill during the last several missions, so his concentration was centered on the striking of ground targets. On 21 May he and Lt. Bob O'Nan attacked a factory and some high tension wires near Berlin. The 352nd returned to the Berlin area on 24 May and engaged enemy targets both in the air and on the ground. While the 328th and 486th FS fought the air battle, the 487th headed earthward and struck hard. Whisner did some "working on the railroad" during which he destroyed seven locomotives and damaged three others. By use of his machine guns he also accounted for the destruction of a railroad station, one gun emplacement, and a tugboat.

On 29 May the 352nd FG escorted formations of B-24s to targets deep in Germany, and the Luftwaffe took to the air to meet them. As the air armada passed over Gastrow, the bombers were struck, head-on by a mixed force of at least 40 Me 109s and FW 190s. This attack was observed by pilots of the 487th who quickly peeled off and engaged the enemy fighters while they were regrouping. Lt. Whisner, leading Yellow Flight, flew toward some FW 190s and personally encountered a very aggressive opponent who, upon seeing Whisner's approach, turned to meet him. The melee was on! The two pilots sparred with each other from 26,000 feet down to the deck before Lt. Whisner got the advantage. Despite his constant maneuvering, the adversary could not turn inside Whisner's Mustang to fire. As the planes thundered above the treetops, Whisner found a clear shot and hit the 190 with six quick bursts which caused the aircraft to roll, plummet to earth, and explode upon impact.

The next mission to Germany, on 30 May, took the 352nd FG to the target of Magdeburg, a city which was known to contain petroleum and aircraft plants. The Luftwaffe rose in strength to protect the city and its vital facilities. The Bluenosers quickly encountered heavy resistance, and the air battles which ensued fully involved all three of the 352nd's squadrons. The tally at the end of the fighting showed the 352nd with a score of 13 1/2-2-1 prior to returning to Bodney Airfield. One of the downed enemy aircraft was credited on the basis of one half for Lt. Whisner and one half for Captain George Preddy, which raised Whisner's score to 6 1/2 enemy aircraft destroyed.

During the first week of June, the 352nd escorted bombers on missions to strike targets in France and Belgium. Beginning on 6 June 1944 (D-Day), and for the next two weeks, the Bluenosers were assigned bombing and strafing missions in support of the invasion forces with concentration near and along the front. On 7 June Bill Whisner, Lt. Robert Hall, and Captain Preddy made multiple firing passes on a German convoy near Vernuil. This attack resulted in the destruction of fifteen vehicles and heavy damage to those remaining. Soon thereafter, Lt. Whisner and his flight returned to the invasion front twice on one busy day, striking and shattering a column of German reinforcements during the morning mission and flying escort for a dive bombing mission in the evening.

Upon the completion of flying on 13 June, Lt. Whisner was handed orders which sent him on a well earned leave to the United States. He returned to the 352nd FG in late September and soon realized that the tempo of air operations had significantly changed during his absence. Specifically, the Luftwaffe had become conspicuous by its absence, and people were wondering if the German air force was finished. From 28 September through 31 October, the 352nd did not record the damage or destruction of a single enemy aircraft, and newly promoted Captain Whisner undoubtedly wondered if his second tour of combat duty was really necessary. However, during a mission on 1 November, a few German fighters were engaged, and Lt. Bill Gerbe of the 486th FS shared the destruction of an Me 262 jet aircraft with a pilot of the 56th FG. Few would have guessed that this minor engagement would be followed the next day by one of the largest air battles to occur over Europe during World War II.

The mission of 2 November was a powerful strike against the German petroleum facilities at Merseburg. The bomber force numbered over 1,100 aircraft and was escorted by a huge armada of fighters. The mission plan called for some diversionary strikes designed to conceal the real target, but the Luftwaffe was not fooled and concentrated its fighter force on Merseburg. The initial skirmishes began as the first bomber force, which consisted of the

3rd Air Division and its escorts, passed the IP. Major engagements were joined about twenty minutes later, at approximately 1230, when the bombers of the 1st Air Division arrived over the IP escorted by Mustangs of the 20th, 352nd, 359th and 364th Fighter Groups.

The 352nd made contact with the enemy fighters at a point east of Merseburg where a furious running air battle lasted for some thirty minutes. The 328th FS, led by Major George Preddy, struck first and claimed a score of 25-1-2 for his unit's portion of the action. There were plenty of targets for the 486th and 487th FS, however, and Captain Bill Whisner, leading Blue Flight in his brand new P-51 named "Moonbeam McSwine," scored one of the 487th's eight credits for aircraft destroyed in the air. His flight was at 32,000 feet when he saw a gaggle of 16 Me 109s heading toward the B-17s and led his flight downward in the attack. Bill swung in behind the last flight of Messerschmitts and was lining one of them up in his sights when a Mustang from another group appeared from nowhere and caused him to swerve to avoid a collision. Having lost his first opportunity, he then pulled in behind another 109 and opened fire. The bullets from "Moonbeam's" six fifties ripped into the enemy fighter and tore large chunks of metal away from the fuselage before Whisner saw the aircraft fall away and head to earth trailing a plume of smoke and fire. Lt. Karl Waldron, who had observed the action, confirmed the downing.

The day's combat had been an incredible success for the 8th Fighter Command. Its pilots had destroyed 134 German fighters, probably destroyed 3 and damaged 25. Unfortunately, U.S. losses numbered 40 bombers and 16 fighters. Additionally, the resistance encountered demonstrated that the Luftwaffe was still capable of massing significant aerial combat power, an indication that many more air battles could be anticipated over the skies of Germany. The combat also served as a preview of the 352nd's next major battle, during which Captain Bill Whisner would have his greatest day as a fighter pilot.

On 21 November the 352nd FG again headed to Merseburg as part of the escort force for a huge formation of bombers. The Group found itself heavily engaged with enemy fighters just after the bombers left the target area. The combat action started when elements of the 352nd spotted a formation of enemy fighters flying parallel to the bombers and began the attack. Captain Bill Whisner was leading a flight, which was part of an eight ship formation led by Lieutenant Colonel John C. Meyer, and recalled the action, as follows: "At approximately 1225 hours we saw a gaggle of 50 plus enemy aircraft flying on an interception course to the last box of bombers which had already left the target area. ("Box" refers to the "Box Formation" used by the Bomber Command as a protective measure. It allowed the bombers to provide mutually supporting fire in each element of the larger armada.) We were climbing through 23,000 feet and immediately pushed our throttles "wide open" after the enemy aircraft, closing in behind them at 29,000 feet. Major Preddy, leading a three ship formation from the 328th, was close behind us. The enemy attack force numbered more than 20 aircraft in close formation with six, three ship covering formations flying fairly wide above, to the sides and rear of them. As we approached our adversaries from the rear, the covering flights began to "Split-S" away, which was a cause for our concern. I identified our target aircraft as FW 190s and noted that they all had belly tanks."

Colonel Meyer directed Captain Whisner to attack a straggler on the right and to the rear of the targeted formation. After missing with his initial burst, Whisner closed to within 200 yards of his target and ripped large chunks of metal from the 190 with a well placed burst from his fifties. As the Focke Wulf fell in flames, Captain Whisner turned his attention to another 190, closed and fired from about 150 yards. The enemy aircraft immediately fell away and was hit by another burst of fire from Whisner's guns before it descended in a flat spin and disappeared in layer of haze.

After this second encounter Captain Whisner noted, "At this time the enemy seemed to be worried. I saw two aircraft break away, dive downward and take evasive action. I did not attempt to follow them but stayed with the enemy formation." He then closed in behind a three ship formation which was flying "line abreast," about 50 yards apart. Bill lined up on what he presumed to be the flight leader; before he could fire, the aircraft broke away, and he found himself between the two remaining 190s, at which time he chose to attack the one to his right. Before that pilot could react, Whisner destroyed the 190 with a well placed burst from 100 yards. His wingman, Lt. Karl Waldron, then zoomed in and shot down the other 190.

As Captain Whisner recovered from this combat engagement, another 190 crossed in front of him and paid for this mistake. The 190 was staggered when hit by a deflection shot of 15 to 20 degrees at 200 yards and went down in flames. Moments later Whisner saw another 190 going down in smoke and flames and confirmed his wingman's second kill of the day. While watching Waldron's prey plummet toward earth, Bill made a 180 degree turn to the right and got separated from his wingman. Nevertheless, he again went after the enemy formation and noted that the main portion was still intact but with only two aircraft from the covering flight remaining in sight. While approaching the main formation, Whisner picked out his next victim and hit the 190 with a short burst which sent the aircraft into a spin. This aircraft disappeared into the haze and was claimed as a "probable." No sooner had he broken off from this firing run than another enemy aircraft appeared. Whisner's fire caused this aircraft to explode and was listed as Bill's fourth confirmed kill of the day.

The explosion in flight of the German aircraft must have caused the enemy pilots to consider their situation more closely, and the order was obviously given to all enemy pilots to drop their "belly tanks" and break formation. Seconds after the jettisoned fuel tanks were observed, Captain Whisner found three aircraft on his tail and successfully climbed away from them. Upon reaching 25,000 feet he spotted an enemy aircraft hot on the tail of a Mustang. He tried a deflection shot at the FW 190 and missed, but apparently the enemy pilot was so intent on gunning down his target that he failed to see "Moonbeam McSwine" closing on him. At a point blank range of 50 yards, Captain Whisner opened fire and "hosed" the 190s engine and cockpit areas. The aircraft went down in a vertical dive and crashed. After recording his fifth downed aircraft of the day, Captain Whisner joined up with his wingman and Colonel John Meyer and headed home to Bodney. This had been a great day for the 352nd Fighter Group "Bluenosers" over all and Captain William T. Whisner, Jr. in particular. The Group had claimed a total of 22 1/2-2-6 during the battle with no losses of their own.

The next several flights over Germany were uneventful, but during the mission of 27 November the Luftwaffe once again rose to meet the Bluenosers. In the battle which followed, the 352nd claimed a score of 17-0-1 in the air before diverting to strafing runs against numerous trains. Captain Whisner was active in both engagements by downing two enemy aircraft and damaging two trains and a barge. The downed aircraft brought Bill Whisner's credits to fourteen confirmed enemy aircraft destroyed and two "probables."

Three weeks later the ground war in Europe was thrown into turmoil and confusion when the Germans launched their powerful counterattack in the Ardennes Forest, which is best known as "The Battle of the Bulge." Under the cover of some of the worst weather experienced on the continent, the German army rolled back the Allied lines, and the issue appeared seriously in doubt until the 101st Airborne Division made its heroic stand at Bastogne. The weather finally began to clear, and the Allies were able to initiate aerial operations in the "Bulge" area on 23 December. The 9th Air Force was given the mission to support the battlefront on this date, and the 8th Fighter Command attached the 352nd and 361st FGs to the 9th in the Belgium area to fulfill this tactical requirement. This arrangement led to one of the 352nd's most spectacular and impressive victories of the war. The aerial action which took place on 1 January 1945 resulted in honors for the 487th FS, and decorations for several of its pilots. Captain Bill Whisner was one of the heroic pilots who participated in this most unusual aerial battle, which took place when the Luftwaffe launched yet another major attack.

Their aerial offensive was designed to destroy the Allied Tactical Air Forces which were now based in Holland and Belgium. The German High Command believed their Ardennes offensive could be salvaged if the Allied planes in the area were destroyed and the plan, entitled "OPERATION BODENPLATTE," was initiated in the early morning hours of New Year's Day. (A second interpretation is that this operation, planned by General Adolf Galland against his better judgement but under Hitler's orders, was necessary to protect the German troops during their retreat to the Rhine after the Battle of the Bulge.) At least 800 heavily armed fighters and fighter-bombers headed westward toward sixteen targeted Allied airfields. The attack was quite successful against some, and nearly 200 friendly planes were destroyed. Heaviest hit was the Royal Air Force which lost 120 aircraft. The Luftwaffe suffered even heavier losses of an estimated 300 aircraft and over 200 irreplaceable pilots. The staggering enemy losses shattered the hopes of the Luftwaffe planners and can best be attributed to several factors which included accidents and Allied anti-aircraft fire, along with swift and decisive action on the part of Allied fighter pilots. Without a doubt the most significant air battle of the day took place over Asch Airfield, which served as testimony to the training and individual heroism of the American pilots who were involved.

Asch Airfield (Y-29), located in Belgium, had become the home of the 366th Fighter Group of the 9th Air Force and the temporarily attached 352nd Fighter Group from the 8th Air Force. Asch was a forward airstrip just 15 miles from the German lines which had none of the comforts to which the Bluenosers had become so well accustomed at Bodney Airfield in England. The transition from warm buildings to tents with camp stoves created a problem for both the pilots and ground crews, with the greatest impact on the latter. Each squadron of the 352nd had a full complement of pilots in Belgium, but only a small percentage of the ground crews and maintenance personnel was relocated forward with the squadron's aircraft. The 352nd FG arrived at Asch on 23 December. Conditions in Belgium during the next eight days are best described in "The Legend of Y-29," a brief history of the 487th's stay at Asch Airfield, the author of which is unknown. He wrote: "It was cold in Belgium—much colder than it had been at Bodney. The snow was four feet deep and digging foxholes was a chore as the ground had long been frozen over. But, captain and private, colonel and corporal went to work and made themselves outside, down-under bedrooms. It was a good thing we did, because from the very first night the Nazis paid regular, after sundown visits. Being garrison troops from way back, pilots and ground personnel—especially the groundhogs—were more unnerved by the American ack-ack being thrown up around them than by the enemy planes overhead. Roughly, that was the situation during the week leading up to New Years Day." During those days the Group had shot down a number of German planes, with the 487th doing most of the scoring. "January 1st was cold. It was bitter cold at 0530 when the ground crews, mechanics, armorers and radiomen went to pre-flight the P-51s. The Group was standing ready for a bomber escort mission that morning. By 0800 the planes had all been checked."

Across the field the ground personnel of the 366th FG were performing the same pre-flight chores on their P-47s. The 366th was scheduled for an early morning attack against German positions in the "Bulge" area. Eight Thunderbolts of their 390th FS would be the first friendly aircraft in the air that morning.

The 352nd FG, on the other hand, had been scheduled to take off in the afternoon as part of a 9th AF "maximum effort" attack, several hours after the 366th morning mission. However, the 352nd's acting commander, Lt. Colonel John C. Meyer, had a "gut" feeling that the Germans might try something because of the New Year celebrations and requested permission from General Quesada's 9th Air Force Headquarters to fly an early morning patrol. Permission was granted with the stipulation Meyer "swear" that he would have a full force back on the ground for the afternoon mission. The 487th FS, with Colonel Meyer in the lead, was thus scheduled to take off at 0930 hours.

The Thunderbolts of the 390th FS preceded the Bluenosers into the air by 15 minutes and were setting course for their target area when Lt. Jack Kennedy saw flak bursts north-east of the field. The 390th, led by Captain Lowell Smith, turned the formation to investigate. The P-47 pilots saw a flight of approaching enemy fighters and immediately engaged them. The Thunderbolt attack seemed to momentarily disrupt the German formation, which was heading toward Asch Airfield, even as the 487th Mustangs were taxiing to the run-up area, making final checks and lining up for take-off in two ship flights. Meyer's final pre-take off quip over the radio was "looks like a good day to go Kraut hunting."

The German formation was not deterred for long by the 390th, and the 487th literally had to fight its way into the air. Lt. Colonel Meyer claimed the first downed aircraft as he was still initiating his take off, with the landing gear not completely raised, when he turned slightly to fire at a low flying German plane which was intent upon shooting at the C-47 parked at the side of the field. By the time Captain Bill Whisner's third flight ascended from the runway, the sky was filled with low flying enemy fighters, and his first score of the day occured while he was still in his take-off climb.

Captain Whisner described the chaos: "On the ground, the mechanics, armorers, radio men, the one intelligence officer who came along with the Group, as well as the rest of the pilots, started cheering, and ducking. It was the first time any of them had ever seen a fight over their own airfield. 'Kill the bastards,' roared the armorers of the squadron. They had checked the guns of the squadron's ships that morning and now they were able to see some of the results of their handiwork. They saw plenty from the crowded ditch which had been bulldozed for ground crew protection from aerial attack. For aside from the dogfights which were going on overhead, the "friendly" ack-ack boys surrounding the field were filling the sky with lead. The first 190 Col. Meyer shot down landed just outside the field, and his second, which he bagged some distance away, was seen to go down in flames, too." Bob Powell interjects that the personnel in the ditch were also subject to strafing by the Me 109s and that he is the recent (1997) recipient of one of the many spent German machine gun shell casings which rained down during the strafing runs. He was provided this memento by Jim Lambright of Largo, Florida, who kept the casing after being hit in the neck by it during the action being described.

"Watch Whiz! Watch Whiz!" shouted the group of squadron personnel in the ditch and individual foxholes who had been working that bitterly cold morning. "There goes one!" came a cry, and sure enough, a 190 went hurtling down.

Captain Whisner, who got another 190 as well as two 109s before he landed, wrote the following in his encounter report: "As I pulled my wheels up after taking off, I heard over the radio that there were bandits east of the field. We didn't take time to form up but set course wide open, straight for the bandits. There were a few P-47s mixing it up with the Germans, and as I arrived I ran into about 30 FW 190s at 1,500 feet, and there were many Me 109s above them. I picked out a 190 and pressed the trigger. Nothing happened. I then reached down, turned on my gun switch, and gave him a couple good bursts. As I watched him hit the ground and explode, I felt my aircraft being hit. I broke sharply to the right and up. A 190 was about 50 yards behind me, firing away. As I was turning away from him another P-51 attacked him, and he broke off from his attack on me. I then saw that I had several 20mm holes in each wing and a hit in my oil tank. My left aileron was also out and I was losing oil, but my oil pressure and temperature were steady. Being over friendly territory, I could see no reason for landing immediately, so I turned toward a big dogfight and shortly had another 190 in my sights. After hitting him several times, he (the pilot) tried to bail out, but I gave him a burst as he raised up, and he went in with the plane which exploded. There were several 109s in the vicinity, so I engaged one of them. We fought for five or ten minutes and I finally managed to get behind him. I hit him good, and he tumbled to the ground. At this time I saw 15 to 20 fires from crashed planes. Bandits were reported strafing the field, so I headed for the strip. I saw a 109 strafe the northeast portion of our airfield and started after him. He turned toward me and we made two head-on passes at each other. On the second I hit him in the nose and wings, and the 109 crashed and burned east of the field. After the crash I chased several more bandits, but they evaded into the clouds. By this time my windshield was covered with oil, so I headed back to Asch and landed."

"Moonbeam McSwine" was a mess when Bill landed her, but she had served her pilot very well during one of his greatest missions. Whisner was officially credited with the destruction of four German aircraft during this rather brief engagement. Altogether, the 487th FS destroyed 23 enemy planes, suffered no losses of their own during the battle, and became the only squadron in 8th Air Force to be awarded the Distinguished Unit Citation. After the devastating defeat of 1 January 1945, the Luftwaffe again became scarce, and the 352nd FG had to hunt to find targets. (There was no comment about the fate of the "maximum effort" mission planned for the afternoon of 1 January, but it is doubtful that such a plan remained in effect after the morning's aerial activity.) During the remaining twelve missions which Captain Whisner flew with the 352nd he did not realize a single opportunity to close with an enemy aircraft and completed his European tour of duty with the Bluenosers possessing a personal record of 18 1/2-2-0, with 15 1/2-2-0 the result of aerial combat.

Bill Whisner returned to the United States in March of 1945 and was honorably discharged in September of that year. His tenure as a civilian did not last long, however, as he was recalled to active duty a year after discharge and assigned to the 4th Fighter Group at Andrews Air Base, Maryland. Shortly thereafter he was selected to be an exchange officer and sent to England to fly "Vampires" with the Royal Air Force. This tour of duty extended through the end of 1947, and his next assignment in the United States was with the 56th Fighter Group at Selfridge Field, Michigan.

William T. Whisner, Jr. was promoted to Major in 1951 and given orders transferring him to the famous 4th Fighter Interceptor Wing (FIW) in Korea, and another combat tour, just as the air war was "heating up." The North Korean Air Force (NKAF) had utilized the lull in ground fighting, which occurred during the peace talks, to build up their MiG 15 forces and construct new airfields in North Korea. As it gained in numerical strength the NKAF began aggressive, large scale assaults against the United Nations Air Forces and succeeded in denying our fighter bombers access to "MiG Alley." In a counter move, the Far East Air Force (FEAF) increased its F-86 daylight patrols up to the Yalu River and initiated B-29 "Superfortress" Bomber strikes against the Communist airfields during the night. While the bombing had some effect, it was not as positive as had been hoped, and daylight bombing raids were then ordered against the enemy air bases. The first of these missions caught the Communists by complete surprise and was highly successful; however, subsequent missions turned out quite differently. During the bombing mission of 22 October, one B-29 was shot down by a MiG 15, and the following day matters got much worse.

The Superforts returned to North Korea on 23 October with a 34 aircraft escort of F-86 and F-84 fighters. Disaster struck in the form of approximately 100 MiGs which totally engaged the fighter force while an additional 50 MiGs attacked the bombers. The escort aircraft were significantly outclassed, and the engagement resulted in the loss of three Superforts and one F-84. During the remainder of October, the loss of bombers continued, and it became clear to the FEAF commander that their daylight employment should be discontinued. It was equally obvious that the 4th FIW could not successfully compete with the NKAF due to its limited assets and capabilities and that the F-86 strength in Korea must be immediately increased.

The intensity of the air war extended into November, and Major Whisner was able to contribute to the scoring. During the mission of 8 November, which was a fighter sweep into North Korea, Whisner led a flight of four F-86 "Saber Jets" from the 334th Fighter Interceptor Squadron (FIS). As they approached Sukchon, Whisner spotted a formation of MiG 15s and immediately turned for an engagement. The MiG pilots were apparently oblivious to the F-86s bearing in on them and turned directly in front of the Sabers. Major Whisner opened fire on the last MiG in formation and saw the flashes of numerous hits all over the enemy fighter. Within seconds the stricken aircraft entered a fatal dive and crashed into a small hill 3 miles west of Sukchon.

On the next day Major Whisner, again as a 334th Flight Leader, returned to North Korea and quickly found enemy aircraft. As he arrived over Sinanju, a flight of enemy fighters appeared, and the opposing forces began sparring for position. Bill worked his way to the rear of the formation and chose "Tail End Charlie" as his target. He "fanned" his fire over the MiG and saw hits on the tail, fuselage and wings of the aircraft. An additional burst was fired for good measure, which resulted in the enemy pilot ejecting just before the aircraft started downward. This was his second and last kill while a member of the 334th FIS.

The 51st Fighter Interceptor Wing was directed to convert from their F-84s to the newly arriving F-86Es during the latter part of November. This directive was implemented by transferring an experienced cadre from the 4th FIW which included personnel to assume command positions. Colonel Francis S. Gabreski (one of "The Inner Seven") took command of the 51st FIW on 6 November and was followed by the other pilots selected from the 4th, which included Major Bill Whisner who was assigned as commander of the 25th FIS.

The newly equipped 51st FIW flew its first combat mission on 1 December and recorded successful engagements during the missions of 2 and 4 December. The capabilities of the F-86E permitted the 51st to fly higher than the 4th FIW which was flying earlier model aircraft. The advantage of patrolling at higher altitudes rapidly resulted in the destruction of an increased number of enemy aircraft during December 1951 and January 1952 when the 51st claimed 25 aircraft destroyed as compared to 5 for the more experienced 4th FIW.

Two of the downed aircraft recorded by the 51st FIW in January were credited to the commander of the 25th FIS. Major Whisner destroyed his first enemy aircraft with the new organization during a mission to MiG Alley on 6 January. At about 1540 hours his flight of seven F-86Es arrived in the Wongsong-dong area and immediately engaged four MiG 15s. Whisner led the attack and singled out the formation leader as his prey. His personal action vas over quickly as it only took two short bursts from his six fifties to cause the enemy ircraft to explode. The second credit came five days later near Yongsan-dong. The encoun-er report stated, "While flying #3 position in a flight of three F-86s I sighted two MiG 15s ınd attacked the number two MiG. After firing several short bursts I observed strikes in the ail section, wings and fuselage. The pilot bailed out and the plane crashed in the vicinity of Yongsan-dong." Whisner had chalked up his fourth destroyed enemy aircraft during this tour.

After the beatings experienced in January, the NKAF began operating at higher alti-udes during February and attempted to avoid combat with the F-86Es. The lack of resolve ⁀n the part of the North Korean pilots reduced the number of aerial engagements in MiG Alley, and the Saber pilots claimed only 17 downed aircraft—11 by the 51st FIW and 6 by the 4th FIW—during February. Ironically, it was during this period of limited combat that the U.S. Air Force lost one of its greatest "Aces." Major George A. Davis, the leading Ace in Korea with credit for the destruction of 14 enemy aircraft, was downed and killed in a dogfight which ⁀ook place on 10 February. He was the only member of "The Inner Seven" lost in combat.

At this point in time Major Whisner and Colonel Gabreski were tied with four downed enemy aircraft each. It was only a matter of time until one of them would become the 7th "Jet Ace" of the Korean Conflict. On 20 February 1952 the 51st FIW was operating in the ⁀rea of Uiju with Gabreski and Whisner each leading a flight of four Sabers. Gabreski was the first to spot enemy fighters and led his F-86s after them. He pulled in behind six MiGs which were flying in a strung-out formation, and "Gabby" opened fire at the rearmost, ⁀ausing it to smoke but not lose speed. As Gabreski moved closer to his target, pieces of the aircraft ripped away and crashed into his windshield. He then broke contact to assess the extent of his aircraft damage. Seeing that the smoking aircraft was still maintaining air-speed, and heading toward its sanctuary north of the Yalu River, Major Whisner picked up

Winners of the National Air Races at Dayton, Ohio, September 1953. The Winners shown are: MC at the podium, Tice received 3rd place; Johnson received 2nd place; Whisner won 1st place.

Christmas 1970 at Lakenheath Air Force Base, England. (l to r): Bob Hope, Colonel William T. Whisner and Colonel Frank Gailer

the chase and followed it into Manchuria. After they had gone about 50 miles, the MiG pilot turned in front of Whisner and was hit by three of Bill's machine gun bursts which caused him to "hit the silk."

After his return to the base, Major Whisner learned that Colonel Gabreski had already claimed the MiG as a "probable" and wrote his report so as to change Gabreski's claim to "destroyed." Gabreski, however, would have none of that, and the two pilots were credited with half each, which left the two still tied. Official Air Force records indicated that the aircraft was shot down near Uiju, North Korea, since crossing into Manchuria was forbidden.

The tie only lasted for three more days and ended during a mission to the Sinuiju area. Air battles were already underway when Major Whisner arrived on the scene, and he observed one of the engaged F-86s in real trouble. He immediately headed for the MiG which was attacking Major Don Adams and forced it to break away. As he flew after this MiG, a second came in behind his ship and opened fire. Whisner ignored the attack and continued to pursue his target, opening fire at a range of about 300 yards, causing the MiG pilot to take violent evasive action. The maneuvers did not fool the veteran pilot, and as he closed on the MiG, he again opened fire. The pilot ejected just before the aircraft exploded, making Bill Whisner the 7th Jet Ace of the Korean Conflict. Major Adams, the pilot saved by Whisner's intercession, went on to become the 14th Jet Ace during action in Korea. In addition to 5 1/2 enemy aircraft confirmed as destroyed, Major Whisner also damaged six other MiGs during his combat tour in Korea, which was completed in November of 1952.

His next assignment was at Nellis Air Force Base, Nevada, where he added to his laurels by winning the 1953 Bendix Trophy Race. In August of 1954 Major Whisner was transferred to Randolph AFB, Texas, for two years of staff duty, during which he was selected for attendance at the Royal Air Force Staff College prior to becoming commander of the Tactical Air Command's 494th Fighter Squadron stationed at Chaumont Air Base, France.

He was promoted to Lt. Colonel in March of 1959 and returned to the United States wi 1 assignment as a plans officer at Headquarters, Department of the Air Force.

In June of 1962 Lt. Colonel Whisner was sent to Luke AFB, Arizona, and serve J as commander of a TAC training squadron prior to returning to duty in Washington, D.C. in 1963. He was promoted to Colonel during this assignment and transferred to Germany where he served as Chief of Staff of the 17th Air Force until his retirement from the Air Force on 1 August 1972.

This exceptionally talented and courageous aviator lived quietly with his wife, Jacquetta, in his native state of Louisiana until his death on 21 July 1989 which, of all things, was attributed to a bee sting

Presentation of Flowers to Princess Ann of England immediately following the official opeaning of Lakenhgath Elementary School by the Princess on 11 June 1970. Shown (l to r): unnamed school girl; Major General Bell, Commander of the 3rd Air Force; Princess Anne; Mary Downing, Lady in wait- ing; and Colonel William T. Whisner, C.O. of 48th T.F.W.

Colonel William T. Whisner, Junior
United States Air Force, Retired
SN 0-798190 & 0-39455

Awards And Decorations
Distinguished Service Cross with Two Oak Leaf Clusters
Silver Star Medal
Distinguished Flying Cross with Four Oak Leaf Clusters
Bronze Star Medal
Air Medal with Twelve Oak Leaf Clusters
USAF Commendation Medal with One Oak Leaf Cluster

Service Medals
American Defense Service Medal
American Campaign Medal
European-African-Middle Eastern Campaign Medal with Four Bronze Stars
World War II Victory Medal
Korean Service Medal with Two Bronze Stars
National Defense Service Medal with One Bronze Star
Vietnam Service Medal with Three Bronze Stars
Republic of Vietnam Campaign Medal
USAF Longevity Service Award with One Silver Oak Leaf Cluster

Citations
Presidential Unit Citation
Distinguished Unit Citation

Foreign Decorations
United Nations Service Medal with Two Bronze Stars
Republic of Korea Presidential Unit Citation

Credits For Enemy Aircraft Destroyed During Combat Actions

Date		Aircraft Destroyed	Location
		World War II	
1944	29 January	1 FW 190	Malmady
	30 April	1 FW 190	Clermont-Ferrand
	29 May	1 FW 190	Gustrow
	30 May	1 Me 109	Magdaburg
	2 November	1 Me 109	Merseburg
	21 November	5 FW 190	Merseburg
	27 November	2 Me 109	Hameln
1945	1 January	2 Me 109	Liege
		2 FW 190	Liege
		Korea	
1951	8 November	1 MiG 15	Sukchon
	9 November	1 MiG 15	Sinanju
1952	6 January	1 MiG 15	Wongsong-dong
	11 January	1 MiG 15	Yongsan-dong
	20 February	.5 MiG 15	Uiju
	23 February	1 MiG 15	Tang Won-Dong

SUMMARY: The youngest of "The Inner Seven", Colonel Whisner served as an inspiration to all who knew him during the period of his exciting and dynamic career.

Official Record: 21 Enemy Aircraft Destroyed, 2 Probably Destroyed, 6 Damaged and 3 Destroyed on the ground.

Across: Major George Preddy congratulates Captain William T. Whisner upon "Bill" becoming an "Ace" on 21 November 1944 while assigned to the 352nd Fighter Group, Bodney, England.
Source: Whisner Collection

Epilogue

A t the time of this writing, two of "The Inner Seven" are still alive and enjoying many activities in their retirement years. They were so kind as to review their respective chapters and provide some elements of accuracy as well as words of encouragement. With the exception of LTC Davis, who was killed in action in Korea, the author interviewed each of the others at length and found them to be quite relaxed and modest gentlemen——somewhat of a contradiction to what was anticipated of their level of combat experience, exploits and heroism.

In discussing the preparation and composition of this history with friends and people in the publishing field, several suggested that we attempt to identify the common threads which are woven into, or lie within and throughout the lives of those whom we honor with this text, especially as concerns the question, "What inherent characteristics or elements of heredity, upbringing, or other factors can be attributed to the obvious dedication to and love of country and fellow airmen to the point that they would continuously risk their lives in wartime combat service?" It is our sincere hope that the reader may have been able to glean some insight as to the answer, or answers, to these questions during the reading of the personal life history and professional exploits of each of our heroic patriots as presented.

Our purpose was only to provide an historical text which highlights and records the lives and military careers of the only seven American military aviators to accomplish the feat for which they are honored. Elusive in the quest to determine as many facts as possible concerning each person was the answer to the question having to do with what made each of our heroes such a calm and competent combat leader so early in life and while still honing the skills so necessary to survive and win in the highly dangerous challenges of aerial warfare. This was one element of commonality, but where, when, and how did each learn to lead so well at such a young age and with so little relative experience?

One area which consistently is of interest to the aviation community has to do with air and ground safety. We noted that their were no accidents attributed to these seven aviators, which is remarkable when one considers the type of aircraft and primitive fields and facilities which were utilized in WW II and during the Korean Conflict. Aeronautical skill, concentration, and constant awareness of ground hazards, and proper aircraft functioning obviously were a major part of the personal makeup of each of "The Inner Seven." When one considers the many thousands of hours flown under all types of air and ground conditions, their collective safety record is most amazing and impressive.

Finally, we hope that our efforts will result in two things happening: First, that the memory of the seven men and their exploits, contributions, and personal histories will live, via the written word, in posterity. Second, that the youngsters of our present and future generations will explore the lives of these gallant Americans and emulate the professionalism and devotion to duty, honor, and country so well exemplified by "The Inner Seven."

Appendises

Appendix I

Glossary of Military Terms
and Abbreviations

(The Corporate Name of the Aircraft Manufacturer is Shown in Parenthesis)

A-20	Twin Engine Attack Bomber "Havoc" (Douglas)
AB	Air Base
A/C	Aircraft
Ace	Military pilot with official credit for the air-to-air destruction of 5 enemy aircraft
AD	Air Division
AFB	Air Force Base
ANG	Air National Guard
AT	Advanced Training
AT-6	Advance Training Aircraft "Texan"- also Navy Trainer SNJ (North American Aviation}
"Bandit"	Enemy aircraft
"Betty"	Japanese Twin Engine Bomber G4M (Mitsubishi)
Bf 109	Single Engine German Fighter until 1938, at which time it became the Messerschmitt 109
BG	Brigadier General
"Bounce"	Surprise attack from or against enemy aircraft, generally from above
"Break"	Warning or instruction to make an abrupt turn
BT	Basic Training/Basic Trainer
BT-13	Basic Trainer "Vibrator" (Vultee)
B-17	Four Engine Bomber "Flying Fortress" (Boeing)
B-24	Four Engine Bomber "Liberator" (Consolidated)
B-25	Twin Engine Bomber "Billy Mitchell" (North American)
B-26	Twin Engine Bomber "Marauder" (Martin)
B-29	Four Engine Bomber "Superfortress" (Boeing)
C-47	Twin Engine Transport "Skymaster" (Douglas)
C-54	Four Engine Transport (Douglas)
Capt.	Captain
CAVU	Ceiling and Visibility Unlimited
"Check Out"	Term used for qualification in a designated Aircraft
"Check Six"	A radio warning to one or more pilots to look to their rear for enemy aircraft
Col.	Colonel
D. 520	French Single Engine Fighter (Dewoitine)
DFC	Distinguished Flying Cross
"Dinah"	Twin Engine Japanese Reconnaissance Aircraft (Mitsubishi, Type Shinshitei)
"Dog Fight"	Two or more opposing aircraft engaged in a dedicated aerial engagement
DUC	Distinguished Unit Citation
E/A	Enemy Aircraft
"Ersatz Coffee"	Synthetic coffee developed and used by the Germans during WW II
ETO	European Theater of Operations
FEAF	Far East Air Force
F2F	Navy Single Seat Fighter Trainer, Vintage 1935 (Grumman)
F2H	Navy Fighter "Banshee" (McDonald Douglas)
F-4	Jet Fighter "Phantom" (McDonald Douglas)
F4F	Navy Fighter (Grumman)
F4U	Navy Fighter "Corsair" (Vought)
F9F	Navy Jet Fighter "Panther" (Grumman)
F-80	Jet Fighter "Shooting Star" (Lockheed)
F-84	Jet Fighter "Thunderjet" (Republic)
F-86	Jet Fighter "Sabre Jet" or "Sabre" (North American)
F-94	Jet Fighter "Starfighter" (Lockheed)
F-100	Jet Fighter "Super Sabre" (North American)
FW 190	German Single Engine Fighter (Focke-Wulf)
FBW	Fighter Bomber Wing
FC	Fighter Command

FG	Fighter Group
FEAF	Far East Air Force
FIS	Fighter Interceptor Squadron
FIW	Fighter Interceptor Wing
"Flak"	Antiaircraft Fire
FS	Fighter Squadron
"Gaggle"	A grouping of Aircraft in loose formation
"Glasshouse"	Plexiglas aircraft canopy
"Hamp"	An improved version of the Japanese "Zero" fighter aircraft. (originally nicknamed
"Hap"	after General "Hap" Arnold. His disapproving reaction resulted in the adding of the "m")
"Hat Trick"	The shooting down of three or more aircraft during a single mission
IAS	Indicated Air Speed
IO	Intelligence Officer
IP	Initial Point. used by Bomber Formations to initiate a Bombing Run
IP	Instructor Pilot
JROTC	Junior Reserve Officer Training Corps
Ju 87	Twin Engine German Attack Aircraft (Junkers)
Ju 88	Twin Engine German Medium Bomber (Junkers)
K-13	Suwon Air Base, Korea (51st FIW)
K-14	Kimpo Air Base, Korea (4th FIW)
K-55	Osan Air Base, Korea
Ki-46	Twin Engine Japanese Reconnaissance Aircraft "Dinah" (Mitsubishi)
"Kate"	Japanese Small Bomber and Torpedo Plane, B5N (Nakajima)
KIA	Killed In Action (Pertaining to Personnel)
"Kite"	British vernacular term for aircraft
La-9	Single Engine Russian Fighter which saw limited use against U.S. Forces (Lavochkin)
Leave	Military term for vacation
LCM	U.S. ship-sized landing craft used to transport mechanized vehicles and troops to shore
LRFG	Long Range Fighter Group
Lt.	Lieutenant
Lt. Col.	Lieutenant Colonel
"Lufbery Circle"	An aerial engagement where opposing pilots follow each other in a circle waiting for the enemy to break out and become a target
Luftwaffe	The German Air Force
"Mayday"	Radio transmission by a pilot who has an onboard emergency
Me 109	Single Engine German Fighter (Messerschmitt) Also Bf 109. general usage is Me 109.
Me 110	Twin Engine German Fighter Bomber (Messerschmitt) Also Bf 110, best known as Me 110
Me 262	Twin Engine German Jet Fighter (Messerschmitt)
MiG 15	Single Engine Russian Jet Fighter Flown by the North Korean Air Force
MAG	Marine Air Group
"MiG Alley"	The area over North Korea most frequently used by NKAF pilots to enter South Korea
Maj.	Major
MAS	Marine Air Station
N3N	Single Engine Bi-Wing Navy Trainer "Yellow Peril" (Naval Aircraft Factory, Philadelphia)
NAS	Naval Air Station
NKAF	North Korean Air Force
NORAD	North American Air Defense Command
OLC	Oak Leaf Cluster—each denotes an additional award of the same military medal
"On the Deck"	Flight at tree top level
"Oscar"	Single Engine Japanese Fighter Aircraft used in "Kamikaze" (Suicide) attacks (Nakajima)
P-38	Twin Engine Fighter "Lightning" (Republic)
P-39	Single Engine Fighter "Airacobra" (Bell)
P-40	Single Engine Fighter "Warhawk" (Curtis)
P-47	Single Engine Fighter "Thunderbolt" (Republic)
P-51	Single Engine Fighter "Mustang" (North American)
PT-13	Primary Trainer (Stearman)
PT-17	Primary Trainer (Stearman)
PT-19	Primary Trainer (Fairchild)
PT-22	Primary Trainer (Ryan)
P-36	Single Engine Fighter, Pre-WW II. four saw action at Pearl Harbor

PG	Pursuit Group
PS	Pursuit Squadron
POE	Port of Embarkation
POW	Prisoner of War
PT	Primary Training
RAF	Royal Air Force, Great Britain
RAAF	Royal Australian Air Force
Ramrod	Bomber escort mission
Rodeo	Bomber escourt with bombers as bait to draw enemy up to engage fighter escourt
Rotate	Change of aircraft attitude on take off when the pilot raises the nose to enter flight
ROTC	Reserve Officer Training Corps
R & R	Rest and Recreation
R/V	Rendezvous
"Saber/Saber Jet"	Interchangeable name or designation of the F-86
"Scramble"	Term used to describe rapid mission take off by American Aviation elements
SEA	Southeast Asia
"Spitfire"	British Fighter Aircraft
"Split S"	An aircraft maneuver to change direction and lose altitude by rolling into a dive followed by recovery at the desired altitude
T-33	Jet Training Aircraft "Shooting Star" (Lockheed)
TAC	Tactical Air Command
TFW	Tactical Fighter Wing
"Thunderbolt"	P-47 Fighter, also called "Thunderbomber" when equipped with bomb racks
"The Inner Seven"	Identifies only seven Aces of WW II who became Aces in Jets during the Korean Conflict
"Tony"	Japanese Fighter Aircraft (Kawasaki Hein), Ki-61
Tu-2	Russian Twin Engine Bomber
"Val"	Japanese Attack Aircraft (Dive Bomber) Type 99, D3A1 (Aichi)
"Vampire"	Twin Engine British Fighter FMK1 (de Havilland)
VMF	Marine Corps Fighter Squadron
WADS	Washington Air Defense Sector
WW I & WW II	World War I and World War II
"Zeke"	Nickname for the improved Japanese "Zero" fighter aircraft
"Zero"	The Primary Japanese Fighter Aircraft

NOTE 1: *Military documents and records differ in the designation of certain enemy aircraft. For example, the ME-109, Me-109 and Me 109. The designations used in the text of this book were obtained from the Office of Air Force History as being the correct ones.*

NOTE 2: *"Bronze Star, or Stars" when stated in the listing of individual Service Medals denotes the number of campaign periods that the service member was in the Theater for which awarded, and should not to be confused with the Bronze Star Medal.*

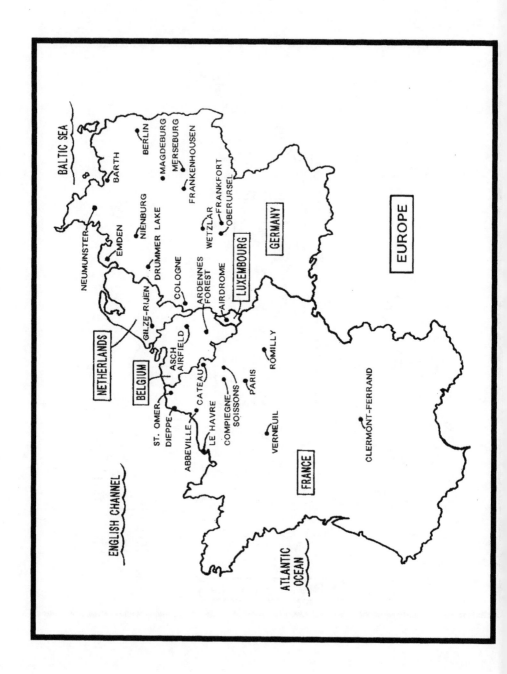

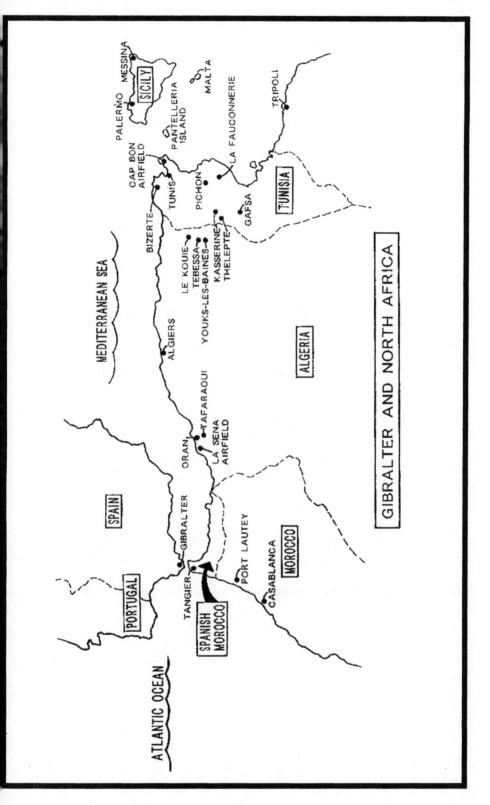

GIBRALTER AND NORTH AFRICA

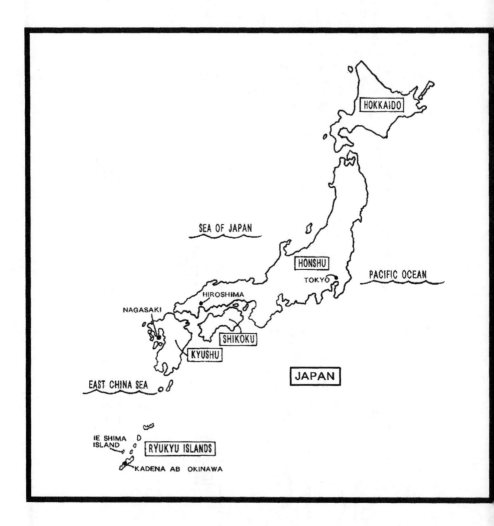

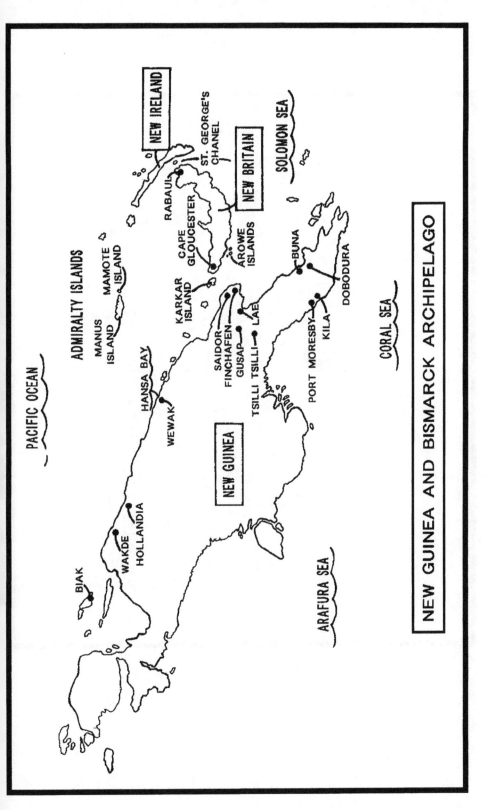

NEW GUINEA AND BISMARCK ARCHIPELAGO

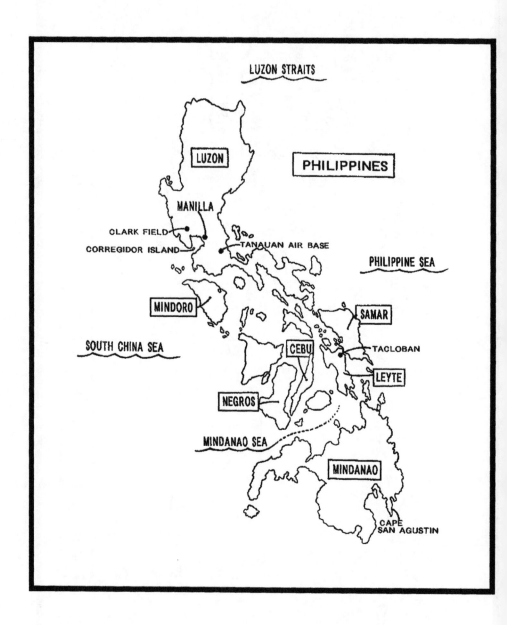

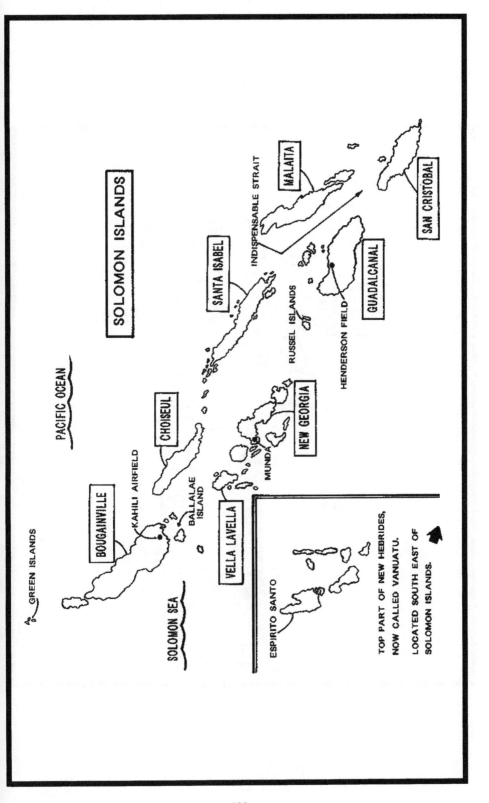

SOLOMON ISLANDS

GREEN ISLANDS

PACIFIC OCEAN

BOUGAINVILLE

KAHILI AIRFIELD

BALLALAE ISLAND

CHOISEUL

SOLOMON SEA

VELLA LAVELLA

MUNDA

NEW GEORGIA

RUSSEL ISLANDS

SANTA ISABEL

INDISPENSABLE STRAIT

MALAITA

SAN CRISTOBAL

GUADALCANAL

HENDERSON FIELD

ESPIRITO SANTO

TOP PART OF NEW HEBRIDES, NOW CALLED VANUATU.

LOCATED SOUTH EAST OF SOLOMON ISLANDS.

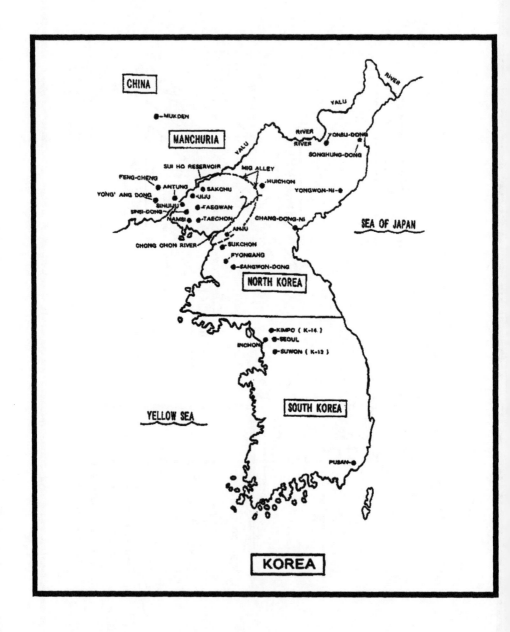

F4U-1 "Corsair"

VMF-214, Espiritu Santo/Turtle Bay

P-40-N "Warhawk"

At Munda Field, New Georgia Island, Flown by 49th Fighter Group

British "Spitfire"

Flown by the U.S. 31st Fighter Group

P-47 "Thunderbolt"

Flown by the 56th, 348th and 413th Fighter Groups

P-51 "Mustang"

Flown by the 4th and 352nd Fighter Groups

F-86 "Saber Jet"

Flown by the 4th and 51st Fighter Interceptor Wings

Printed in the USA
CPSIA information can be obtained
at www.ICGtesting.com
JSHW082228140824
68134JS00016B/782

9 781681 621272